P9-CLP-390

John Adams

A Photo-Illustrated Biography

by Muriel L. Dubois

Consultant:
Anne Decker Cecere
Associate Editor
The Adams Papers
Massachusetts Historical Society

Bridgestone Books
an imprint of Capstone Press
Mankato, Minnesota

Bridgestone Books are published by Capstone Press
151 Good Counsel Drive, P.O. Box 669, Mankato, Minnesota 56002
http://www.capstone-press.com

Library of Congress Cataloging-in-Publication Data
Dubois, Muriel L.
    John Adams : a photo-illustrated biography / by Muriel L. Dubois.
    p. cm.—(Photo-illustrated biographies)
    Summary: A biography of the second president of the United States, covering his
childhood, his marriage to Abigail Smith, and his role in creating the United States
government.
    Includes bibliographical references and index.
    ISBN 0-7368-1606-2 (hardcover)
    1. Adams, John, 1735–1826—Juvenile literature. 2. Adams, John, 1735-1826—Pictorial
works—Juvenile literature. 3. Presidents—United States—Biography—Juvenile literature.
[1. Adams, John, 1735–1826. 2. Presidents.] I. Title. II. Series.
E322 .D83 2003
973.4′4′092—dc21   2002008973

Editorial credits
Erika Shores, editor; Karen Risch, product planning editor; Linda Clavel, cover designer
    and interior illustrator; Alta Schaffer, photo researcher

Photo credits
Bettmann/CORBIS, 20
Hulton/Archive by Getty Images, 10
Hulton/Archive by Getty Images/Stock Montage, Inc., cover, 4
North Wind Picture Archives, 6, 14, 16, 18
Stock Montage, Inc., 8, 12

1 2 3 4 5 6 08 07 06 05 04 03

Table of Contents

John Adams

John Adams was the second president of the United States. He is called a Founding Father. The Founding Fathers worked to create the United States.

John Adams was a lawyer, a writer, and a statesman. As a lawyer, he helped people protect themselves and their property. In the 1700s, Great Britain ruled the 13 American colonies. The king of Great Britain taxed the people living in the American colonies. John argued that the new taxes were unfair.

As a statesman, John played an important role in the birth of the United States. He helped write the Declaration of Independence. He also wrote the Massachusetts Constitution. John represented the United States in Europe. He was the United States' first vice president.

John worked to create the United States.

Family and School

John Adams was born in Braintree, Massachusetts, on October 30, 1735. Later, Braintree was renamed Quincy. His father, John, was a farmer and a shoemaker. People called him Deacon John. Deacons, like John's father, helped ministers at churches. John's mother, Susanna, cared for their home and helped with the farm.

John had two younger brothers, Peter and Elihu. As the oldest son, John was urged to go to school. His father wanted John to study to become a minister.

At first, John did not like school. He wanted to farm like his father. Deacon John insisted John go to Harvard College in Boston. John obeyed his father. He graduated from Harvard in 1755. But John did not want to become a minister.

The house in this photograph is part of the Adams National Historical Park in Quincy, Massachusetts. It is one of the houses John lived in during his lifetime.

"The Revolution was effected before the war commenced. The Revolution was in the minds and hearts of the people."
–John, in a letter written on February 13, 1818

John the Lawyer

John did not know what to do after college. While he decided, he taught school for two years. John then studied law. John began by reading law books. He then studied with a lawyer named James Putnam. John became a lawyer in 1758.

The next year, John met Abigail Smith. They married in 1764 and settled in Braintree. He and Abigail soon started a family. They would have five children, Abigail (Nabby), Susanna, John Quincy, Charles, and Thomas. Susanna died in 1770.

In 1770, John became the lawyer for several British soldiers. The king had sent soldiers to America to make sure colonists followed his tax laws. One day, the British soldiers fought with people in Boston. The soldiers killed five men. John defended the soldiers even though he did not agree with the king's tax laws. John believed every person should have a fair trial.

The fight between the British soldiers and the people in Boston became known as the Boston Massacre.

"Yesterday the Greatest question was decided, which ever was debated in America,...that those united Colonies, are, and of right ought to be free and independent States...."
–John, in a letter to his wife Abigail, July 3, 1776

Declaring Freedom

In 1774, a group of colonists gathered in Philadelphia. The colonists wanted to make their own laws. John attended this Continental Congress.

The Congress decided America should break free from Great Britain. Great Britain did not want to lose its colonies. In 1775, the Revolutionary War (1775–1783) began. The Congress wrote the Declaration of Independence in 1776. John helped write this document. It told Great Britain that the colonies wanted to be free.

The colonists needed help to fight the war. In 1777, the Congress sent John to France to ask for money and soldiers.

John returned to the United States in 1779. He wrote the Massachusetts Constitution. This document made new laws for Massachusetts. The people of Massachusetts adopted their constitution in 1780. They would no longer follow Great Britain's laws.

Members of the Continental Congress wrote the Declaration of Independence.

Sent to Europe

In 1779, the Continental Congress sent John back to Europe. John took his sons John Quincy and Charles with him. John had three important tasks. He again asked France for help. He asked the Netherlands to lend money to the colonists. He also planned a peace treaty with Great Britain.

John stayed in Europe for eight years. He missed his family, but he completed his tasks. French soldiers went to fight in America. The Netherlands lent the colonists money.

In 1783, John, Benjamin Franklin, and John Jay signed the official peace treaty between the United States and Great Britain. The Revolutionary War was over. The United States was free. In 1784, Abigail and Nabby sailed to Europe. In 1785, Congress made John a diplomat to Great Britain. Diplomats are officials who form friendships between countries.

John became a diplomat to Great Britain in 1785. This illustration shows John meeting with King George III.

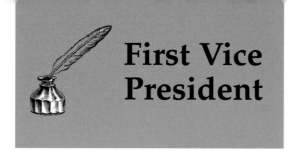

First Vice President

In 1788, John and Abigail returned to the United States. John and Abigail were happy to be back in Massachusetts. But they did not stay there for long. The United States needed leaders like John. The country was free, but it needed a new government.

In March 1789, George Washington became the first president of the United States. John was elected vice president. New York City was the first capital of the United States. John and Abigail moved to New York.

In 1790, Philadelphia was named the U.S. capital. John and Abigail moved to another new home. Abigail soon returned to their Quincy farm. Her health was not good. She worried about their farm. John continued his work as vice president for six more years. He visited Quincy when he could.

George Washington was sworn in as the first president of the United States in 1789.

"...I pray Heaven to bestow the best of Blessings on this House and all that shall hereafter inhabit it. May none but honest and wise Men ever rule under this roof. "
–John, in a letter written to Abigail, November 2, 1800

President Adams

George Washington retired after eight years as president. In 1796, John was elected president. Thomas Jefferson became vice president.

John faced difficult problems as president. Great Britain and France were at war. Their ships often attacked U.S. ships. John sent men to Europe to work for peace. He asked Congress to create the U.S. Navy. The Navy protected U.S. ships.

John sent diplomats to other countries. John's son, John Quincy, was a diplomat to Prussia in Europe.

In 1800, Washington, D.C. became the country's capital. The government built a house for the president. John was the first president to live in the White House. John and Abigail lived in the White House for only a few months.

John was the first president to live in the White House in Washington, D.C.

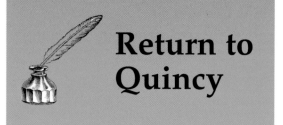

Return to Quincy

In December 1800, the U.S. people elected Thomas Jefferson president. John was president for ten more weeks. His government work was nearly done.

John was ready to go home. John and Abigail missed their farm. John had lived away from Massachusetts for 22 years. He gave all that time to help create the United States.

Abigail left Washington, D.C. a few weeks before John. She went to Quincy to prepare their home. John finished his work as president.

Early on March 4, 1801, John Adams left Washington, D.C. John did not watch Thomas Jefferson become president. John was angry that he lost the election to Jefferson. He and Jefferson had once been friends. But they often disagreed on how the U.S. government should operate.

Abigail wrote many letters to John during their lifetime. People study their letters today to learn about what life was like during the late 1700s.

Later Years

John and Abigail were happy on their farm. At first, John rested and wrote letters. John Quincy then urged his father to write about his life.

In 1802, John began writing his life story. He described the work of the Continental Congress. He told of his years in Europe. John worked on his book for five years, but he never finished it.

John also became friends with Thomas Jefferson again. They wrote more than 150 letters to each other.

On October 28, 1818, Abigail died. John was saddened by her death. John's son Thomas and his family moved to the farm. They helped care for John and the land. John continued to write and organize his papers. He knew they were important for history.

John Adams died on July 4, 1826. It was the 50th anniversary of the Declaration of Independence.

John was 90 years old when he died on July 4, 1826.

Fast Facts about John Adams

 The United States Post Office honored John Adams with stamps showing his portrait in 1938 and 1986.

 John Adams was also the father of a U.S. president. John Quincy Adams became the sixth U.S. president.

 Just before he died, John Adams said, "Thomas Jefferson survives." He did not know his friend had died on the same day, just hours before.

Dates in John Adams' Life

1735—John is born in Braintree, Massachusetts.

1751–1755—John attends Harvard College.

1758—John becomes a lawyer.

1764—John marries Abigail Smith.

1770—John defends British soldiers in Boston Massacre trials.

1774–1777—John attends the Continental Congress in Philadelphia.

1776—John helps write the Declaration of Independence.

1779—John writes the Massachusetts Constitution.

1783—John signs the peace treaty with Great Britain.

1789—John is elected the first vice president of the United States.

1796—John is elected the second president of the United States.

1802–1807—John writes the story of his life.

1818—Abigail Adams dies.

1826—John dies on July 4. Thomas Jefferson dies on the same day.

Words to Know

constitution (kon-stuh-TOO-shuhn)—the system of laws in a country that states the rights of the people and the powers of the government
Continental Congress (KON-tuh-nen-tuhl KONG-griss)—leaders from the 13 original American colonies that served as the American government from 1774 to 1789
deacon (DEE-kuhn)—an officer of a church who helps the minister
diplomat (DIP-loh-matt)—a person sent by a government to represent it in another country
massacre (MASS-uh-kur)—the killing of a large number of people
statesman (STAYTSS-muhn)—a person skilled at dealing with issues relating to government

Read More

Burgan, Michael. *John Adams: Second U.S. President.* Revolutionary War Leaders. Philadelphia: Chelsea House, 2001.

Gaines, Ann Graham. *John Adams: Our Second President.* Our Presidents. Chanhassen, Minn.: Child's World, 2002.

Santella, Andrew. *John Adams.* Profiles of the Presidents. Minneapolis: Compass Point Books, 2003.

Useful Addresses

Adams National Historical Park
135 Adams Street
Quincy, MA 02169-1749

The Adams Papers
Massachusetts Historical Society
1154 Boylston Street
Boston, MA 02215

Internet Sites

Track down many sites about John Adams.
Visit the FACT HOUND at *http://www.facthound.com*

IT IS EASY! IT IS FUN!

1) Go to *http://www.facthound.com*
2) Type in: 0736816062
3) Click on "FETCH IT" and FACT HOUND will
   find several links hand-picked by our editors.

Relax and let our pal FACT HOUND do the research for you!

Index

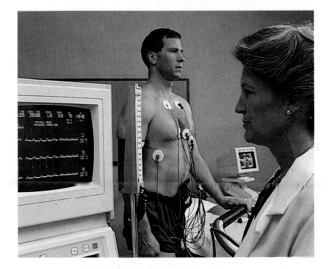

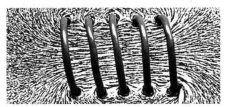

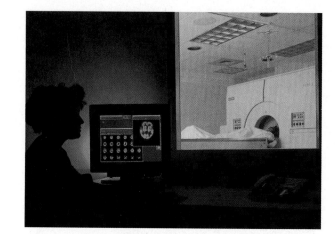

PREFACE

A Fifth Edition?

By the fifth edition of an algebra-based physics text, one might expect that the author has at last gotten it right.

I hope the earlier editions weren't all that wrong. The idea of a new edition is to improve, to bring in material, and perhaps to delete material that makes the book longer but isn't all that useful. All these things have been done:

Physics. Physics itself may not change all that rapidly, but over the span of a few years, there may be some new discoveries to include, such as

- planets revolving around distant stars
- information gathered by the Hubble Space Telescope
- updates in particle physics and cosmology (e.g., age of universe).

Pedagogy. One aspect of physics that is changing fairly rapidly is research on how students learn. As a result, this new edition contains some new elements:

Conceptual Examples, an average of 2 or 3 per chapter, are each a sort of brief Socratic question and answer. It is intended that readers will be stimulated by the questions to think, or reflect, and come up with a response—before reading the Response given. Here are a few:

- Velocity vs. acceleration (Chapter 2)
- What exerts the force on a car? (Chapter 4)
- Apple and the wagon (reference frames and projectile motion, Chapter 3)
- Which object rolls down a plane faster? (Chapter 8)
- Finger on a full straw (Chapter 10)
- Suction (Chapter 10)
- Boiling pasta (Chapter 14)
- Electric shielding/safety from lightning (Chapter 16)
- Which part of the photo is the reflection? (Chapter 23).

Estimating Examples, also a new feature of this edition, are intended to show how to make order-of-magnitude estimates even when the data are scarce, even when you might never have guessed that any result was possible at all.

Problem Solving has not been slighted in the least. There are many new worked-out Examples and here are some highlights:

- Air bags (2-10)
- Bungee jumper (6-14)
- Computer hard drive (8-4)
- Loudspeaker (11 7)
- Photocopier (16-5)
- Age of archeological bone (30-10).

Some of the new Examples have replaced older less useful ones. Many other Examples have been improved by more detailed reasoning, by displaying more mathematical steps, and by improving the ambience to make them more real-world and so more inviting and interesting.

New problems have been added and many of the old ones have undergone change.

Example Titles. Examples of all three types (including Conceptual and Estimating) now have titles (for fun and for easy reference).

Emphasized Equations. The great laws of physics are emphasized not only by setting them off, but also by giving them a marginal note in capitals and in a box. The equations that express the great laws, as well as the major equations that one just can't do without, are emphasized with a tan screen.

New Topics in this fifth edition include (these are only a few)
- Rolling motion (Chapter 8)
- Work in rotational motion ($W = \tau\theta$) (Chapter 8)
- v and a for simple harmonic motion (Chapter 11)
- Highway mirages (Chapter 24)
- Hubble Space Telescope (several places)
- Higgs Boson, Symmetry (explained), Supersymmetry (Chapter 32).

Diagrams. There are many more diagrams (over 200 new ones, for an increase of 20 percent), a lot of them to go with Examples and with Problems. Many of the old diagrams have been improved with more realistic backgrounds and figures, and more detail, and the use of photorealistic art.

Photographs. Many of the chapter opening photos now have vectors or other analysis superimposed on them—to give students a richer feeling for the physics. These are visual images of physics that will be fixed in the students' minds.

Many new and interesting photos have been added in the text to bring home the usefulness of physics, a few of which are: diffusion, images in spherical mirrors, depth of field with a camera lens, Hubble Space Telescope, and DNA X-ray diffraction.

Applications. Relevant applications of physics to everyday life and to biology, medicine, architecture, geology, and other fields has always been a strong feature of this book, and continues to be. Among other things, they answer the students' question, "Why study physics?" New applications have been added (and a few older ones dropped), some of which are

- Elevator and counterweight (Chapter 4)
- Shielding (Chapters 16 and 20)
- Dry cell (Chapter 18)
- Aurora borealis (Chapter 20)
- Induction stove (Chapter 21)
- TV and radio antennas (Chapter 22)
- CD player, laser and disk (Chapter 28)
- Smoke detectors (Chapter 29)

and some already mentioned earlier such as airbags, bungee jumping, photocopiers, highway mirages, and computer hard drives.

Revised Physics. No topic, no paragraph in this book was overlooked in the search to improve the clarity of the presentation. Many changes and clarifications have been made, both small and not so small. Here are just a few of the more important ones:

- New tables of typical lengths, times, masses (Chapter 1) and voltages (Chapter 17)
- Chapter 2: rearranged presentation of displacement, velocity, and reference frames
- New diagrams to aid understanding of velocity and acceleration (Chapter 2)
- Unit conversion moved to Chapter 1
- Relative velocity moved to end of Chapter 3
- Simplified introduction to Newton's second law (Chapter 4)
- Simple machines: pulley (Chapter 4), lever (Chapter 9), hydraulic lift (Chapter 10)
- New Section: "Car rounding a curve" (Chapter 5)
- Period and frequency introduced earlier (Chapter 5)
- Work and energy reworked in general, and potential energy especially dealt with in more detail (Chapter 6)
- Angular momentum simplified a bit, especially vector aspects (Chapter 8)
- More formulas for moment of inertia (Fig. 8-20)
- Rotating reference frames, inertial forces, and Coriolis removed from Chapter 8 to an Appendix
- Greatly simplified vertical spring derivation (Chapter 11)
- Energy transported by waves simplified, with more difficult parts in optional Sections (Chapters 11 and 12)
- Speed of light measurement moved from Chapter 23 on Optics to Chapter 22 on EM waves
- Magnifying glass reworked (Chapter 23)
- Relativistic momentum reworked and in more detail (Chapter 26)
- New energy state diagrams for complex atoms (Chapter 28)
- New results in elementary particle physics and cosmology (Chapters 32 and 33).

Page Layout: Complete Derivations. Serious attention has been paid to how each page was formatted, especially for page turns. Great effort has been made to keep important derivations and arguments on facing pages. Thus readers don't have to turn back to check. More importantly, throughout the book, readers see before them, on two facing pages, an important slice of physics. On rare occasions when an argument related to a particular figure requires a page turn, that figure is repeated after the page turn so readers won't have to look back.

Deletions. With all of these additions, something had to go to keep the book from getting too long. Some new Examples simply replaced less interesting old ones. The treatment of quite a few topics was shortened and some were simply dropped. Here are some of the deletions: derived vs. base units; operational definitions (general details); section on "Laws or Definitions" dropped (kept a tiny bit earlier in Chapter 4); vector nature of angular quantities (greatly shortened); Reynolds number, sedimentation, Stokes' equation; flow in tubes (halved); Olber's paradox.

Scope of this Book

This book is written for students. The two motivating factors are to give students a thorough understanding of the basic concepts of physics and, by means of interesting applications, to prepare them to use physics in their own lives and professions. In particular, this book is written for students who are taking a one-year introductory course in physics that uses algebra and trigonometry but not calculus. Many of these students have as their main interest biology, (pre)medicine, architecture, technology, or the earth and environmental sciences. This book contains a wide range of applications to these and other fields, as well as to everyday life. These applications answer that common student query, "Why must I study physics?" The answer, of course, is that physics comes into play in all these fields very importantly, and here they can see how. Physics is all about us. Indeed, it is the goal of this book to help students see the world through eyes that know physics.

Before the applications must come the physics. And this new edition, even more than previous editions, aims to explain physics in a readable and interesting manner that is accessible and clear. It aims to teach students by anticipating their needs and difficulties, but without oversimplifying.

General Approach

This book offers an in-depth presentation of physics, and retains the basic approach of the earlier editions. Rather than using the common, dry, dogmatic approach of treating topics formally and abstractly first, and only later relating the material to the students' own experience, my approach is to recognize that physics is a description of reality and thus to start each topic with concrete observations and experiences that students can directly relate to. Then we move on to the generalizations. Not only does this make the material more interesting and easier to understand, but it is closer to the way physics is actually practiced.

I have sought, where possible, to present the basic concepts of physics in their historical and philosophic context.

As mentioned above, this book includes a wide range of examples and applications from other fields: biology, medicine, architecture, technology, earth sciences, the environment, and daily life. Some applications serve only as examples of physical principles. Others are treated in depth, with whole Sections devoted to them (among these are the study of medical imaging systems, constructing arches and domes, and the effects of radiation). But applications do not dominate the text—this is, after all, a physics book. They have been carefully chosen and integrated into the text so as not to interfere with the development of the physics but rather illuminate it. You won't find essay sidebars here. The applications are integrated right into the physics. Even when an application gets a separate Section all to itself, it is directly tied to the physics just studied. To make it easy to spot these applications, a new *Physics Applied* marginal note has been added.

Mathematics can be an obstacle to student understanding. To avoid frightening students with an initial chapter on mathematics, I have instead incorporated many important mathematical tools, such as addition of vectors and trigonometry, directly in the text where first needed. In addition, the appendices contain a review of many mathematical topics such as algebra and geometry, as well as dimensional analysis. A few advanced topics are also given an Appendix: Rotating frames of reference, Inertial forces, Coriolis effect; Gauss's law; Galilean and Lorentz transformations.

It is necessary, I feel, to pay careful attention to detail, especially when deriving an important result. I have aimed at including all steps in a derivation, and have tried to make clear which equations are general, and which are not, by explicitly stating the limitations of important equations in brackets next to the equation, such as

$$x = x_0 + v_0 t + \frac{1}{2} a t^2. \qquad \text{[constant acceleration]}$$

Difficult language, too, can hinder understanding: and I have tried to write in a relaxed style, avoiding jargon, and often talking directly to the students. New or unusual terms are carefully defined when first used.

Color is used pedagogically to bring out the physics. Different types of vectors are given different colors (see the chart on page xxiii). There are many new diagrams to illustrate new Examples (and old ones too) and to enrich the text and problems. The fifth edition features new and revised art—including new photorealistic art, more illustrations to accompany the in-text Examples and end-of-chapter problems, and dozens of new photos.

Problem Solving

Strong attention is given to problem solving. Learning how to approach and solve problems is a basic part of a physics course, and is a highly useful skill in itself. Solving problems is also important because the process brings understanding of the physics. Scattered throughout the book are special Sections and special Boxes devoted to how to approach the solving of problems. Many are found in the early chapters, where students first begin wrestling with problem solving; but many are also found later in the book, throughout mechanics, and in electricity, for example, where problem solving is an emphasized issue, as well as in thermodynamics and in optics. These Problem Solving Boxes provide a summary of how to approach problem solving. They do *not* provide a prescription to be followed. Hence they are often placed *after* a few Examples have been done, as a sort of summary of how we have been approaching Problems.

Over 400 Examples are fully worked out in the text. In this new edition, there are three types of Examples: regular worked Examples, Estimating Examples, and Conceptual Examples. The regular Examples are fully worked out in the text, and most are accompanied by analytical drawings. These Examples are designed to help students develop problem-solving skills and range from simple to fairly complicated. Estimating Examples encourage student analysis and understanding by using "back of the envelope" estimations as a problem-solving technique; they increase awareness of the power of analytical thinking. Conceptual Examples, in contrast to numerical problem solving and the application of formulas, challenge students to explore the basic concepts that are fundamental to understanding physics. Many Examples are taken from everyday life and aim at being realistic applications of physics principles.

There are over 3100 end-of-chapter exercises, including more than 700 questions that require verbal answers based on an understanding of the concepts, and about 2400 problems involving mathematical calculation.

Each chapter contains a large group of problems arranged by Section and graded according to difficulty: level I problems are simple, usually plug-in types, designed to give students confidence; level II are normal problems, requiring more thought and often the combination of two different concepts; level III are the most difficult and serve as a challenge to superior students. The arrangement by Section number means only that those problems depend on material up to and including that Section: earlier material may also be relied upon. The ranking of problems by difficulty (I, II, III) is intended only as a guide.

I suggest that instructors assign a significant number of the level I and level II problems, and reserve level III problems to stimulate the best students. Although most level I problems may seem easy, they help to build self-confidence—an important part of learning, especially in physics.

Each chapter also contains a group of "General Problems" which are unranked and not arranged by Section number.

Answers to odd-numbered problems are given at the back of the book. Throughout the text, *Système International* (SI) units are used. Other metric and British units are defined for informational purposes.

Organization

The general outline of this new edition retains a traditional order of topics: mechanics (Chapters 1 to 12), including vibrations, waves, and sound, followed by kinetic theory and thermodynamics (Chapters 13 to 15), electricity and magnetism (Chapters 16 to 22), light (Chapters 23 to 25), and modern physics (Chapters 26 to 33). Nearly all topics customarily taught in introductory physics courses are included here.

The tradition of beginning with mechanics is sensible, I believe, because it was developed first, historically, and because so much else in physics depends on it. Within mechanics, there are various ways to order topics, and this book allows for considerable flexibility. I prefer, for example, to cover statics after dynamics, partly because many students have trouble with the concept of force without motion. Besides, statics is a special case of dynamics—we study statics so that we can prevent structures from becoming dynamic (falling down)—and that sense of being at the limit of dynamics is intuitively helpful. Nonetheless statics (Chapter 9) can be covered earlier, if desired, before dynamics, after a brief introduction to vectors. Another option is light, which I have placed after electricity and magnetism and EM waves. But light could be treated immediately after the chapters on waves (Chapter 11 and 12). Special relativity (Chapter 26), which is located along with the other chapters on modern physics, could instead be treated along with mechanics—say, after Chapter 7.

Not every chapter need be given equal weight. Whereas Chapter 4 or Chapter 21 might require $1\frac{1}{2}$ to 2 weeks of coverage, Chapter 12 or 22 may need only $\frac{1}{2}$ week.

The book contains more material than can be covered in most one-year courses, so instructors have flexibility in choice of topics. Sections marked with a star (asterisk) are considered optional (if not covered in class, they can be a resource for later study). These Sections contain slightly more advanced physics material, often material not usually covered in typical courses, and/or interesting applications. They contain no material needed in later chapters (except perhaps in later optional Sections). This does not imply that all nonstarred sections must be covered: there still remains considerable flexibility in the choice of material. For a brief course, all optional material could be dropped as well as major parts of Chapters 10, 12, 19, 22, 28, 29, 32, and 33, as well as selected parts of Chapters 7, 8, 9, 15, 21, 24, 25, and 31.

Thanks

More than 60 physics professors provided direct feedback on every aspect of the text: organization, content, figures, and suggestions for new Examples and Problems. These reviewers for this fifth edition are listed below. I owe each of them a debt of gratitude:

David B. Aaron (South Dakota State University)
Zaven Altounian (McGill University)
Atam P. Arya (West Virginia University)
David E. Bannon (Chemeketa Community College)
Jacob Becher (Old Dominion University)
Michael S. Berger (Indiana University, Bloomington)
Donald E. Bowen (Stephen F. Austin University)
Neal M. Cason (University of Notre Dame)
H. R. Chandrasekhar (University of Missouri)
Ram D. Chaudhari (SUNY—Oswego)
K. Kelvin Cheng (Texas Tech University)
Lowell O. Christensen (American River College)
Mark W. Plano Clark (Doane College)
Irvine G. Clator (UNC, Wilmington)
Scott Cohen (Portland State University)
Lattie Collins (East Tennessee State University)
Sally Daniels (Oakland University)
Jack E. Denson (Mississippi State University)
Eric Dietz (California State University, Chico)
Paul Draper (University of Texas, Arlington)
Miles J. Dresser (Washington State University)
F. Eugene Dunnam (University of Florida)
Gregory E. Francis (Montana State University)
Philip Gash (California State University, Chico)
J. David Gavenda (University of Texas, Austin)
Grant W. Hart (Brigham Young University)
Melissa Hill (Marquette University)
Mark Hillery (Hunter College)
Hans Hochheimer (Colorado State University)
Alex Holloway (University of Nebraska, Omaha)

James P. Jacobs (University of Montana)
Larry D. Johnson (Northeast Louisiana University)
David Lamp (Texas Tech University)
Paul Lee (University of California, Northridge)
Daniel J. McLaughlin (University of Hartford)
Victor Montemeyer (Middle Tennessee State Univ.)
Dennis Nemeschansky (USC)
Robert Oakley (University of Southern Maine)
Robert Pelcovits (Brown University)
Brian L. Pickering (Laney College)
T.A.K. Pillai (University of Wisconsin, La Crosse)
Michael Ram (University of Buffalo)
David Reid (Eastern Michigan University)
Charles Richardson (University of Arkansas)
Lawrence Rowan (UNC, Chapel Hill)
Roy S. Rubins (University of Texas, Arlington)
Thomas Sayetta (East Carolina University)
Neil Schiller (Ocean County College)
Juergen Schroeer (Illinois State University)
Marc Sher (College of William and Mary)
James P. Sheerin (Eastern Michigan University)
Donald Sparks (Los Angeles Pierce College)
Michael G. Strauss (University of Oklahoma)
Harold E. Taylor (Stockton State University)
Michael Thoennessen (Michigan State University)
Linn D. Van Woerkom (Ohio State University)
S. L. Varghese (University of South Alabama)
Robert A. Walking (University of Southern Maine)
Lowell Wood (University of Houston)
David Wright (Tidewater Community College)

I am grateful also to all those physicist-reviewers of the earlier editions:

Narahari Achar (Memphis State University)
William T. Achor (Western Maryland College)
Arthur Alt (College of Great Falls)
Zaven Altounian (McGill University)
John Anderson (University of Pittsburgh)
Subhash Antani (Edgewood College)
Sirus Aryainejad (Eastern Illinois University)
Charles R. Bacon (Ferris State University)
Arthur Ballato (Brookhaven National Laboratory)
Gene Barnes (California State U., Sacramento)
Isaac Bass
Paul A. Bender (Washington State University)
Joseph Boyle (Miami–Dade Community College)
Peter Brancazio (Brooklyn College, CUNY)
Michael E. Browne (University of Idaho)
Michael Broyles (Collin County Community College)

Anthony Buffa (Cal Poly S.L.O.)
David Bushnell (Northern Illinois University)
Albert C. Claus (Loyola University of Chicago)
Lawrence Coleman (Univ. of California, Davis)
Waren Deshotels (Marquette University)
Frank Drake (Univ. of California, Santa Cruz)
Miles J. Dresser (Washington State University)
Ryan Droste (The College of Charleston)
Frank A. Ferrone (Drexel University)
Len Feuerhelm (Oklahoma Christian University)
Donald Foster (Wichita State University)
Philip Gash (California State University, Chico)
Simon George (California State Univ., Long Beach)
James Gerhart (University of Washington)
Bernard Gerstman (Florida International Univ.)
Charles Glashausser (Rutgers University)

Hershel J. Hausman (Ohio State University)
Laurent Hodges (Iowa State University)
Joseph M. Hoffman (Frostburg State University)
Peter Hoffmann-Pinther (U. of Houston–Downtown)
Fred W. Inman (Mankato State University)
M. Azad Islan (State Univ. of New York—Potsdam)
James P. Jacobs (Seattle University)
Gordon Jones (Mississippi State University)
Rex Joyner (Indiana Institute of Technology)
Sina David Kaviani (El Camino College)
Joseph A. Keane (St. Thomas Aquinas College)
Kirby W. Kemper (Florida State University)
Sanford Kern (Colorado State University)
James E. Kettler (Ohio University–Eastern Campus)
James R. Kirk (Edinboro University)
Alok Kuman (State Univ. of New York—Oswego)
Sung Kyu Kim (Macalester College)
Amer Lahamer (Berea College)
Clement Y. Lam (North Harris College)
Peter Landry (McGill University, Montreal)
Michael Lieber (University of Arkansas)
Bryan H. Long (Columbia State College)
Michael C. LoPresto (Henry Ford Com. College)
James Madsen (University of Wisconsin, River Falls)
Ponn Mahes (Winthrop University)
Robert H. March (University of Wisconsin–Madison)
David Markowitz (University of Connecticut)
E. R. Menzel (Texas Tech University)
Robert Messina
David Mills (College of the Redwoods)
George K. Miner (University of Dayton)
Marina Morrow (Lansing Community College)
Ed Nelson (University of Iowa)
Gregor Novak (Indiana Univ./Purdue Univ.)
Roy J. Peterson (University of Colorado–Boulder)
Frederick M. Phelps (Central Michigan University)

T. A. K. Pillai (University of Wisconsin–La Crosse)
John Polo (Edinboro University of Pennsylvania)
W. Steve Quon (Ventura College)
John Reading (Texas A&M)
William Riley (Ohio State University)
Larry Rowan (University of North Carolina)
R. S. Rubins (University of Texas, Arlington)
D. Lee Rutledge (Oklahoma State University)
Hajime Sakai (Univ. of Massachusetts at Amherst)
Ann Schmiedekamp (Penn State U., Ogontz Campus)
Mark Semon (Bates College)
Eric Sheldon (University of Massachusetts–Lowell)
K. Y. Shen (California State University, Long Beach)
Joseph Shinar (Iowa State University)
Thomas W. Sills (Wilbur Wright College)
Anthony A. Siluidi (Kent State University)
Michael A. Simon (Housatonic Community College)
Upindranath Singh (Embry-Riddle)
Michael I. Sobel (Brooklyn College)
Thor F. Stromberg (New Mexico State University)
James F. Sullivan (University of Cincinnati)
Kenneth Swinney (Bevill State Community College)
John E. Teggins (Auburn Univ. at Montgomery)
Colin Terry (Ventura College)
Jagdish K. Tuli (Brookhaven National Laboratory)
Kwok Yeung Tsang (Georgia Institute of Technology)
Paul Urone (CSU, Sacramento)
Jearl Walker (Cleveland State University)
Jai-Ching Wang (Alabama A&M University)
John C. Wells (Tennessee Technological)
Gareth Williams (San Jose State University)
Thomas A. Weber (Iowa State University)
Wendall S. Williams (Case Western Reserve Univ.)
Jerry Wilson (Metropolitan State College at Denver)
Peter Zimmerman (Louisiana State University)

I owe special thanks to Irv Miller for working out all the problems and for managing the team that also worked out the problems, each checking the others, and finally, producing the answers at the back of the book as well as producing the Solutions Manual.

I am grateful to Paul Draper, Robert Pelcovits, Gregory E. Francis, and James P. Jacobs, who inspired many of the Conceptual Examples, as well as suggestions for Questions and Problems. I wish also to thank Professors Howard Shugart, John Heilbron, Joe Corny, and Roger Falcone for helpful discussions, and for hospitality at the University of California, Berkeley, Physics Department. Thanks also to Prof. Tito Arecchi at the Istituto Nazionale di Ottica, Florence, Italy, and to the staff of the Institute for the History of Science, Florence, for their kind hospitality.

Finally, I am most grateful to the many people at Prentice Hall with whom I worked on this project, especially Susan Fisher, Marilyn Coco, David Chelton, Tim Bozik, Gary June, Kathleen Schiaparelli, Richard Foster, Patrice Van Acker and Dave Riccardi. And special thanks to Paul Corey for guiding this project at every stage with clarity and that rare gift of "getting things done," and to Ray Mullaney, whose high level of dedication through edition after edition has helped make this a clear and accurate book. The final responsibility for all errors lies with me, of course. I welcome comments and corrections.

Douglas C. Giancoli

Supplements

For the Instructor

Instructor's Solutions Manual by Irvin A. Miller *Print version*
(0-13-627985-6); *Electronic Versions:* Windows (0-13-627993-7);
Macintosh (0-13-628009-9)
Contains detailed, worked solutions to every problem in the text by Irv
Miller of Drexel University.

Answers to Questions
Prepared by Michelle Rallis and Kurt Reibel of The Ohio State University,
Columbus and Gordon Aubrecht of The Ohio State University, Marion,
this supplement contains answers to all end-of-chapter questions.

Transparency Pack (0-13-628041-2)
Includes 400 four-color transparencies—nearly twice the number of images
as the previous edition.

Test Item File by Bo Lou (0-13-628017-X)
Over 2,400 multiple-choice test questions—30% new! Many new conceptual problems have been added for the Fifth Edition.

Prentice Hall Custom Test
Windows (0-13-628025-0); Macintosh (0-13-628033-1)
Based on the powerful testing technology developed by Engineering Soft-
ware Associates, Inc. (ESA); Prentice Hall Custom Test allows instructors to
create and tailor exams to their own needs. With the Online Testing Program,
exams can also be administered online and data can then be automatically
transferred for evaluation. A comprehensive desk reference guide is included along with online assistance.

For the Student

Student Study Guide by Joseph Boyle (0-13-627944-9)
Complements the strong pedagogy in Giancoli's text with overviews, topic
summaries and exercises, key phrases and terms, self-study exams, and questions for review of each chapter.

MCAT Study Guide by Joseph Boone (0-13-627951-1)
A thoroughly revised study resource that references all of the physics topics
on the MCAT to the appropriate sections in the text. Additional review,
review questions, and problems are provided.

Physics on the Internet: A Student's Guide
by Andrew Stull and Carl Adler (0-13-890153-8)
The perfect tool to help students take advantage of the *Physics: Principles
and Applications, Fifth Edition* Web page. This useful resource gives clear
steps to access Prentice Hall's regularly updated physics resources, along with
an overview of general navigation strategies. Available FREE for students
when purchased in a special package with Giancoli's text.

**Prentice Hall/*The New York Times*
Themes of theTimes—Physics**
This unique newspaper supplement brings together a collection of the latest physics-related articles from the pages of *The New York Times.*

Media Supplements

Interactive Journey through Physics by Cindy Schwarz, Vassar College,
CD-ROM for Windows and Macintosh, ©1997 (0-13-254103-3)
Whether your students are interested in exploring fascinating physics concepts, improving their grades, or reviewing for the MCAT, *Interactive Journey through Physics* will augment the traditional learning experiences of lecture, lab, and text.

Interactive Physics Player Workbook by Cindy Schwarz,
Windows book/disk (0-13-667312-0); Macintosh book/disk (0-13-477670-4)
An easy way to use *Interactive Physics* in your courses, this highly interactive workbook/disk package contains 40 simulation projects of varying degrees of difficulty. Each contains a physics review, simulation details, hints, explanation of results, math help, and a self test.

Physics Explorer Runtime Version by LOGAL,
Windows (0-13-627969-4); Macintosh (0-13-627977-5)
Tailored for use with Giancoli's text, *Physics Explorer Runtime Version* contains simulations of over 100 problems and examples directly from Giancoli's text. Students can conduct experiments, interactively record results on a spreadsheet, and generate graphs using each of ten independent learning models:
Particle Mechanics—One Body, Two Body, Gravity, and Harmonic Motion
Wave Mechanics—Waves, Ripple Tank, Diffraction
Electricity and Magnetism—One Body Electrodynamics, AC/DC Circuits, Electrostatics.

Presentation Manager CD-Rom
This CD-ROM contains all the text art and videos from the Physics You Can See video tape as well as additional lab and demonstration videos and animations from the *Interactive Journey through Physics* CD-ROM.

Physics: Principles and Applications Web Site
http://www.prenhall.com/giancoli
Features include practice tests with on-line feedback/grading keyed to the text.

Physics You Can See *Videos* (0-205-12393-7)
Each two- to five-minute segment demonstrates a classical physics experiment. Includes 11 segments such as "Coin and Feather" (acceleration due to gravity); "Monkey & Gun" (projectile motion); "Swivel Hips" (force pairs); and "Collapse a Can" (atmospheric pressure).

NOTES TO STUDENTS AND INSTRUCTORS ON THE FORMAT

1. Sections marked with a star (*) are considered optional. They can be omitted without interrupting the main flow of topics. No later material depends on them except possibly later starred sections. They may be fun to read though.

2. The customary conventions are used: symbols for quantities (such as m for mass) are italicized, whereas units (such as m for meter) are not italicized. Boldface (**F**) is used for vectors.

3. Few equations are valid in all situations. Where practical, the limitations of important equations are stated in square brackets next to the equation. The equations that represent the great laws of physics are displayed with a tan background, as are a few other equations that are so useful that they are indispensable.

4. The number of significant figures (see Section 1–4) should not be assumed to be greater than given: if a number is stated as (say) 6, with its units, it is meant to be 6 and not 6.0 or 6.00.

5. At the end of each chapter is a set of questions that students should attempt to answer (to themselves at least). These are followed by problems which are ranked as level I, II, or III, according to estimated difficulty, with level I problems being easiest. These problems are arranged by Section, but problems for a given Section may depend on earlier material as well. There follows a group of General Problems, which are not arranged by Section nor ranked as to difficulty. Questions and problems that relate to optional Sections are starred.

6. Being able to solve problems is a crucial part of learning physics, and provides a powerful means for understanding the concepts and principles of physics. This book contains many aids to problem solving: (a) worked-out Examples and their solutions in the text, which are set off with a vertical blue line in the margin, and should be studied as an integral part of the text; (b) special "Problem-solving boxes" placed throughout the text to suggest ways to approach problem solving for a particular topic—but don't get the idea that every topic has its own "techniques," because the basics remain the same; (c) special problem-solving Sections (marked in blue in the Table of Contents); (d) marginal notes (see below), many of which refer to hints for solving problems, in which case they are so indicated; (e) problems themselves at the end of each chapter (see point 5 above); (f) some of the worked-out Examples are Estimation Examples, which show how rough or approximate results can be obtained even if the given data are sparse (see Section 1–7).

7. Conceptual Examples look like ordinary Examples but are conceptual rather than numerical. Each proposes a question or two, which hopefully starts you to think and come up with a response. Give yourself a little time to come up with your own response before reading the Response given.

8. Marginal notes: brief notes in the margin of almost every page are printed in blue and are of four types: (a) ordinary notes (the majority) that serve as a sort of outline of the text and can help you later locate important concepts and equations; (b) notes that refer to the great laws and principles of physics, and these are in capital letters and in a box for emphasis; (c) notes that refer to a problem-solving hint or technique treated in the text, and these say "Problem Solving"; (d) notes that refer to a physics application in the text or an Example, and these say "Physics Applied."

9. This book is printed in full color. But not simply to make it more attractive. The color is used above all in the figures, to give them greater clarity for our analysis, and to provide easier learning of the physical principles involved. The table on the next page is a summary of how color is used in the figures, and shows which colors are used for the different kinds of vectors, for field lines, and for other symbols and objects. These colors are used consistently throughout the book.

NOTES ON USE OF COLOR

Vectors

A general vector	
resultant vector (sum) is slightly thicker	
components of any vector are dashed	
Displacement ($\mathbf{D}$, $\mathbf{r}$)	
Velocity ($\mathbf{v}$)	
Acceleration ($\mathbf{a}$)	
Force ($\mathbf{F}$)	
Force on second or	
third object in same figure	
Momentum ($\mathbf{p}$ or $m\mathbf{v}$)	
Angular momentum ($\mathbf{L}$)	
Angular velocity ($\boldsymbol{\omega}$)	
Torque ($\boldsymbol{\tau}$)	
Electric field ($\mathbf{E}$)	
Magnetic field ($\mathbf{B}$)	

Electricity and magnetism

Electric field lines	
Equipotential lines	
Magnetic field lines	
Electric charge (+)	+ or ● +
Electric charge (−)	− or ● −

Electric circuit symbols

Wire	
Resistor	
Capacitor	
Inductor	
Battery	

Optics

Light rays	
Object	
Real image (dashed)	
Virtual image (dashed and paler)	

Other

Energy level (atom, etc.)	
Measurement lines	⊢—1.0 m—⊣
Path of a moving object	
Direction of motion or current	

How many aspects of Physics do you see in this photograph? (Partial answer given upside down at bottom of photograph.)

Motion, speed, momentum, work, energy, structures and forces within them (why do they stay up?), rotational motion, torque, angular momentum, fluids, drag forces, friction, wave motion. . . .

INTRODUCTION 1

P hysics is the most basic of the sciences. It deals with the behavior and structure of matter. The field of physics is usually divided into the areas of motion, fluids, heat, sound, light, electricity and magnetism, and the modern topics of relativity, atomic structure, condensed-matter physics, nuclear physics, elementary particles, and astrophysics. We will cover all these topics in this book, beginning with motion (or mechanics, as it is often called). But before we begin on the physics itself, let us take a brief look at how this overall activity called "science," including physics, is actually practiced.

FIGURE 1-1 Aristotle is the central figure (dressed in blue) at the top of the stairs (the figure next to him is Plato) in this famous Renaissance portrayal of *The School of Athens*, painted by Raphael around 1510. Also in this painting, considered one of the great masterpieces in art, are Euclid (drawing a circle at the lower right), Ptolemy (extreme right with globe), Pythagoras, Sophocles, and Diogenes.

1-1 Science and Creativity

The principal aim of all sciences, including physics, is generally considered to be the search for order in our observations of the world around us. Many people think that science is a mechanical process of collecting facts and devising theories. This is not the case. Science is a creative activity that in many respects resembles other creative activities of the human mind.

Observation

Let's take some examples to see why this is true. One important aspect of science is *observation* of events. But observation requires imagination, for scientists can never include everything in a description of what they observe. Hence, scientists must make judgments about what is relevant in their observations. As an example, let us consider how two great minds, Aristotle (384–322 B.C.; Fig. 1–1) and Galileo (1564–1642; Fig. 2–15), interpreted motion along a horizontal surface. Aristotle noted that objects given an initial push along the ground (or on a tabletop) always slow down and stop. Consequently, Aristotle believed that the natural state of an object is to be at rest. Galileo, in his reexamination of horizontal motion in the early 1600s, imagined that if friction could be eliminated, an object given an initial push along a horizontal surface would continue to move indefinitely without stopping. He concluded that for an object to be in motion was just as natural as for it to be at rest. By inventing a new approach, Galileo founded our modern view of motion (more details in Chapters 2, 3, and 4), and he did so with a leap of the imagination. Galileo made this leap conceptually, without actually eliminating friction.

Theories are creations

Observation and careful experimentation and measurement are one side of the scientific process. The other side is the invention or creation of *theories* to explain and order the observations. Theories are never derived directly from observations. They are inspirations that come from the minds of human beings. For example, the idea that matter is made up of atoms (the atomic theory) was certainly not arrived at because someone observed atoms. Rather, the idea sprang from creative minds. The theory of relativity, the electromagnetic theory of light, and Newton's law of universal gravitation were likewise the result of human imagination.

The great theories of science may be compared, as creative achievements, with great works of art or literature. But how does science differ from these other creative activities? One important difference is that science requires *testing* of its ideas or theories to see if their predictions are borne out by experiment.

Testing a theory

Although the testing of theories can be considered to distinguish science from other creative fields, it should not be assumed that a theory is "proved" by testing. First of all, no measuring instrument is perfect, so exact confirmation cannot be possible. Furthermore, it is not possible to test a theory for every possible set of circumstances. Hence a theory can never be absolutely "proved." In fact, theories themselves are generally not perfect—a theory rarely agrees with experiment exactly, within experimental error, in every single case in which it is tested. Indeed, the history of science tells us that long-held theories are sometimes replaced by new ones. The process of one theory replacing another is an important subject in the philosophy of science; we can discuss it here only briefly.

*Theory
acceptance*

A new theory is accepted by scientists in some cases because its predictions are quantitatively in much better agreement with experiment than those of the older theory. But in many cases, a new theory is accepted only if it explains a greater *range* of phenomena than does the older one. Copernicus's Sun-centered theory of the universe (Fig. 1–2b), for example, was originally no more accurate than Ptolemy's Earth-centered theory (Fig. 1–2a) for predicting the motion of heavenly bodies (Sun, Moon, planets). But Copernicus's theory had consequences that Ptolemy's did not, such as predicting the moonlike phases of Venus. A simpler (or no more complex) and richer theory, one which unifies and explains a greater variety of phenomena, is more useful and beautiful to a scientist. And this aspect,

FIGURE 1–2 (a) Ptolemy's geocentric view of the universe. Note at the center the four elements of the ancients: Earth, water, air (clouds around the Earth), and fire; then the circles, with symbols, for the Moon, Mercury, Venus, Sun, Mars, Jupiter, Saturn, the fixed stars, and the signs of the zodiac. (b) An early representation of Copernicus's heliocentric view of the universe with the Sun at the center. (See Chapter 5.)

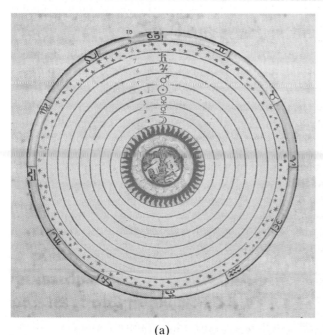

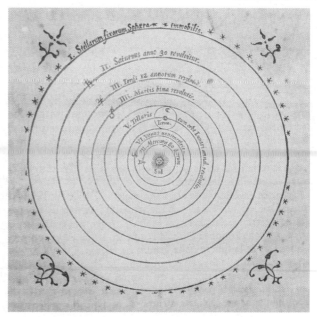

(a)

(b)

as well as quantitative agreement, plays a major role in the acceptance of a theory.

An important aspect of any theory is how well it can quantitatively predict phenomena, and from this point of view a new theory may often seem to be only a minor advance over the old one. For example, Einstein's theory of relativity gives predictions that differ very little from the older theories of Galileo and Newton in nearly all everyday situations. Its predictions are better mainly in the extreme case of very high speeds close to the speed of light. In this respect, the theory of relativity might be considered as mere "fine-tuning" of the older theory. But quantitative prediction is not the only important outcome of a theory. Our view of the world is affected as well. As a result of Einstein's theory of relativity, for example, our concepts of space and time have been completely altered, and we have come to see mass and energy as a single entity (via the famous equation $E = mc^2$). Indeed, our view of the world underwent a major change when relativity theory came to be accepted.

1–2 Physics and Its Relation to Other Fields

For a long time science was more or less a united whole known as natural philosophy. Not until the last century or two did the distinctions between physics and chemistry and even the life sciences become prominent. Indeed, the sharp distinction we now see between the arts and the sciences is itself but a few centuries old. It is no wonder then that the development of physics has both influenced and been influenced by other fields. For example, the notebooks (Fig. 1–3) of Leonardo da Vinci, the great Renaissance artist, researcher, and engineer, contain the first references to the forces acting within a structure, a subject we consider as physics today; but then, as now, it has great relevance to architecture and building. Early work in electricity that led to the discovery of the electric battery and electric current was done by an eighteenth-century physiologist, Luigi Galvani (1737–1798). He noticed the twitching of frogs' legs in response to an electric spark and later that the muscles twitched when in contact with two dissimilar metals (Chapter 18). At first this phenomenon was known as "animal electricity," but it shortly became clear that electric current itself could exist in the absence of an animal. Later, in the 1930s and 1940s, a number of scientists trained as physicists became interested in applying the ideas and techniques of physics to problems in microbiology. Among the most prominent were Max Delbrück (1906–1981) and Erwin Schrödinger (1887–1961). They hoped, among other things, that studying biological organisms might lead to the discovery of new unsuspected laws of physics. Alas, this hope has not been realized; but their efforts helped give rise to the field we now call molecular biology, which has resulted in a dramatic increase in our understanding of the genetics and structure of living beings.

You do not have to be a research scientist in, say, medicine or molecular biology to be able to use physics in your work. A zoologist, for example, may find physics useful in understanding how prairie dogs and other animals can live underground without suffocating. A physical therapist will do a more effective job if aware of the principles of center of gravity and the action of forces within the human body. A knowledge of the operating principles of optical and electronic equipment is helpful in a variety of fields. Life scientists and architects alike will be interested in the nature of heat loss and gain in human beings and the resulting comfort or discomfort. Architects them-

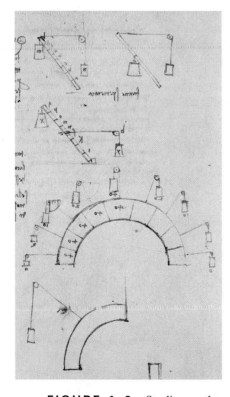

FIGURE 1–3 Studies on the forces in structures by Leonardo da Vinci (1452–1519).

FIGURE 1–4 (a) This Greek temple in Paestum, Italy, was built 2500 years ago, and still stands. (b) Collapse of the Hartford Civic Center in 1978, just two years after it was built.

selves may never have to calculate, for example, the dimensions of the pipes in a heating system or the forces involved in a given structure to determine if it will remain standing (Fig. 1–4). But architects must know the principles behind these analyses in order to make realistic designs and to communicate effectively with engineering consultants and other specialists. From the aesthetic or psychological point of view, too, architects must be aware of the forces involved in a structure—for instability, even if only illusory, can be discomforting to those who must live or work in the structure. Indeed, many of the features we admire in the architecture of the past three millennia were introduced not for their decorative effect but rather for practical purposes. The development of the arch as a means to span a space and at the same time support a heavy load will be discussed in Chapter 9, where we will see that the pointed, or Gothic, arch was not originally a decorative device but a technological development of considerable importance.

The list of ways in which physics relates to other fields is extensive. In the chapters that follow we will discuss many such applications as we carry out our principal aim of explaining basic physics.

1–3 Models, Theories, and Laws

When scientists are trying to understand a particular set of phenomena, they often make use of a **model**. A model, in the scientific sense, is a kind of analogy or mental image of the phenomena in terms of something we are familiar with. One example is the wave model of light. We cannot see waves of light as we can water waves. But it is valuable to think of light as if it were made up of waves, because experiments indicate that light behaves in many respects as water waves do.

The purpose of a model is to give us an approximate mental or visual picture—something to hold onto—when we cannot see what actually is happening. Models often give us a deeper understanding: the analogy to a known system (for instance, water waves in the above example) can suggest new experiments to perform and can provide ideas about what other related phenomena might occur.

Models

You may wonder what the difference is between a theory and a model. Sometimes the words are used interchangeably. Usually, however, a model is relatively simple and provides a structural similarity to the phenomena being studied, whereas a **theory** is broader, more detailed, and can give quantitatively testable predictions, often with great precision. Sometimes, as a model is developed and modified and corresponds more closely to experiment over a wide range of phenomena, it may come to be referred to as a theory. The atomic theory is an example, as is the wave theory of light.

Theories (vs. models)

Models can be very helpful, and they often lead to important theories. But it is important not to confuse a model, or a theory, with the real system or the phenomena themselves.

Laws

Scientists give the title **law** to certain concise but general statements about how nature behaves (that energy is conserved, for example). Sometimes the statement takes the form of a relationship or equation between quantities (such as Newton's second law, $F = ma$).

and

To be called a law, a statement must be found experimentally valid over a wide range of observed phenomena. In a sense, the law brings a unity to many observations. For less general statements, the term **principle** is often used (such as Archimedes' principle). Where to draw the line between laws and principles is, of course, arbitrary, and there is not always complete consistency.

principles

Scientific laws are different from political laws in that the latter are *prescriptive*: they tell us how we ought to behave. Scientific laws are *descriptive*: they do not say how nature *should* behave, but rather are meant to describe how nature *does* behave. As with theories, laws cannot be tested in the infinite variety of cases possible. So we cannot be sure that any law is absolutely true. We use the term "law" when its validity has been tested over a wide range of cases, and when any limitations and the range of validity are clearly understood. Even then, as new information comes in, certain laws may have to be modified or discarded.

Scientists normally do their work as if the accepted laws and theories were true. But they are obliged to keep an open mind in case new information should alter the validity of any given law or theory.

1–4 Measurement and Uncertainty

In the quest to understand the world around us, scientists seek to find relationships among the various physical quantities they observe and measure.

We may ask, for example, in what way does the magnitude of a force on an object affect the object's speed or acceleration? Or by how much does the pressure of gas in a closed container (such as a tire) change if the temperature is raised or lowered? Scientists normally try to express such relationships quantitatively, in terms of equations whose symbols represent the quantities involved. To determine (or confirm) the form of a relationship, careful experimental measurements are required, although creative thinking also plays a role.

Accurate measurements are an important part of physics. But no measurement is absolutely precise. There is an uncertainty associated with every measurement. Uncertainty arises from different sources. Among the most important, other than blunders, are the limited accuracy of every measuring instrument and the inability to read an instrument beyond some fraction of the smallest division shown. For example, if you were to use a centimeter ruler to measure the width of a board (Fig. 1–5), the result

FIGURE 1–5 Measuring the width of a board with a centimeter ruler. Accuracy is about ±1 mm.

Every measurement has an uncertainty

could be claimed to be accurate to about 0.1 cm, the smallest division on the ruler. The reason is that it is difficult for the observer to interpolate between the smallest divisions, and the ruler itself may not have been manufactured or calibrated to an accuracy very much better than this.

When giving the result of a measurement, it is also important to state the precision, or **estimated uncertainty**, in the measurement. For example, the width of a board might be written as 5.2 ± 0.1 cm. The ± 0.1 cm ("plus or minus 0.1 cm") represents the estimated uncertainty in the measurement, so that the actual width most likely lies between 5.1 and 5.3 cm. The **percent uncertainty** is simply the ratio of the uncertainty to the measured value, multiplied by 100. For example, if the measurement is 5.2 and the uncertainty about 0.1 cm, the percent uncertainty is

Stating the uncertainty

$$\frac{0.1}{5.2} \times 100 = 2\%.$$

Often the uncertainty in a measured value is not specified explicitly. In such cases, the uncertainty is generally assumed to be one or two units (or even three) in the last digit specified. For example, if a length is given as 5.2 cm, the uncertainty is assumed to be about 0.1 cm (or perhaps 0.2 cm). It is important in this case that you do not write 5.20 cm, for this implies an uncertainty on the order of 0.01 cm; it assumes that the length is probably between 5.19 cm and 5.21 cm, when actually you believe it is between 5.1 and 5.3 cm.

Assumed uncertainty

The number of reliably known digits in a number is called the number of **significant figures**. Thus there are four significant figures in the number 23.21 and two in the number 0.062 cm (the zeros in the latter are merely "place holders" that show where the decimal point goes). The number of significant figures may not always be clear. Take, for example, the number 80. Are there one or two significant figures? If we say it is *about* 80 km between two cities, there is only one significant figure (the 8) since the zero is merely a place holder. If it is 80 km within an accuracy of 1 or 2 km, then the 80 has two significant figures. If it is precisely 80 km measured to within ± 0.1 km, then we write 80.0 km.

Which digits are significant?

When making measurements, or when doing calculations, you should avoid the temptation to keep more digits in the final answer than is justified. For example, to calculate the area of a rectangle 11.3 cm by 6.8 cm, the result of multiplication would be 76.84 cm^2. But this answer is clearly not accurate to 0.01 cm^2, since (using the outer limits of the assumed uncertainty for each measurement) the result could be between 11.2 × 6.7 = 75.04 cm^2 and 11.4 × 6.9 = 78.66 cm^2. At best, we can quote the answer as 77 cm^2, which implies an uncertainty of about 1 or 2 cm^2. The other two digits (in the number 76.84 cm^2) must be dropped since they are not significant. As a general rule, *the final result of a multiplication or division should have only as many digits as the number with the least number of significant figures used in the calculation.* In our example, 6.8 cm has the least number of significant figures, namely two. Thus the result 76.84 cm^2 needs to be rounded off to 77 cm^2.

➡ **PROBLEM SOLVING**

Report only the proper number of significant figures in the final result. An extra digit or two can be kept during the calculation.

Similarly, when adding or subtracting numbers, the final result is no more accurate than the least accurate number used. For example, the result of subtracting 0.57 from 3.6 is 3.0 (and not 3.03). Keep in mind when you use a calculator that all the digits it produces may not be significant. When you divide 2.0 by 3.0, the proper answer is 0.67, and not 0.66666666. Digits should not be quoted (or written down) in a result, unless they are truly significant figures. However, to obtain the most accurate result, it is good

Careful: Electronic calculators err with significant figures

practice to keep an extra significant figure or two throughout a calculation, and round off only in the final result. Note also that calculators sometimes give too few significant figures. For example, when you multiply 2.5×3.2, a calculator may give the answer as simply 8. But the answer is good to two significant figures, so the proper answer is 8.0.

Powers of ten
(scientific notation)

It is common in science to write numbers in "powers of ten," or "exponential" notation—for instance 36,900 as 3.69×10^4, or 0.0021 as 2.1×10^{-3}. (For more details, see Appendices A–2 and A–3.) One advantage of exponential notation is that it allows the number of significant figures to be clearly expressed. For example, it is not clear whether 36,900 has three, four, or five significant figures. With exponential notation the ambiguity can be avoided: if the number is known to an accuracy of three significant figures, we write 3.69×10^4, but if it is known to four, we write 3.690×10^4.

CONCEPTUAL EXAMPLE 1–1 **Is the diamond yours?** A friend asks to borrow your precious diamond for a day to show her family. You are a bit worried, so you carefully have your diamond weighed on a scale which reads 8.17 grams. The scale's accuracy is claimed to be ± 0.05 grams. The next day you weigh the returned diamond again, getting 8.09 grams. Is this your diamond?

RESPONSE The scale readings are measurements and do not give the actual value of the mass. Each measurement could have been high or low by up to 0.05 gram or so. The actual mass of your diamond lies most likely between 8.12 grams and 8.22 grams. The actual mass of the returned diamond is most likely between 8.04 grams and 8.14 grams. These two ranges overlap, so there is no reason to doubt that the returned diamond is yours, at least based on the scale readings. (But check the color!)

1–5 | Units, Standards, and the SI System

The measurement of any quantity is made relative to a particular standard or **unit**, and this unit must be specified along with the numerical value of the quantity. For example, we can measure length in units such as inches, feet, or miles, or in the metric system in centimeters, meters, or kilometers. To specify that the length of a particular object is 18.6 is meaningless. The unit *must* be given; for clearly, 18.6 meters is very different from 18.6 inches or 18.6 millimeters.

Standard of length (meter)

The first real international standard was the **meter** (abbreviated m) established as the standard of **length** by the French Academy of Sciences in the 1790s. In a spirit of rationality, the standard meter was originally chosen to be one ten-millionth of the distance from the Earth's equator to either pole,[†] and a platinum rod to represent this length was made. (This turns out to be, very roughly, the distance from the tip of your nose to the tip of your longest finger, with arm and hand stretched out horizontally.) In 1889, the meter was defined more precisely as the distance between two finely engraved marks on a particular bar of platinum–iridium alloy. In 1960, to provide greater precision and reproducibility, the meter was redefined as 1,650,763.73 wavelengths of a particular orange light emitted by

---

[†]Modern measurements of the Earth's circumference reveal that the intended length is off by about one-fiftieth of 1 percent. Not bad!

the gas krypton 86. In 1983 the meter was again redefined, this time in terms of the speed of light (whose best measured value in terms of the older definition of the meter was 299,792,458 m/s, with an uncertainty of 1 m/s). The new definition reads: "The meter is the length of path traveled by light in vacuum during a time interval of 1/299,792,458 of a second."[†]

British units of length (inch, foot, mile) are now defined in terms of the meter. The inch (in.) is defined as precisely 2.54 centimeters (cm; 1 cm = 0.01 m). Other conversion factors are given in the table on the inside of the front cover of this book.

Table 1–1 presents some characteristic lengths, from very small to very large.

The standard unit of **time** is the **second** (s). For many years, the second was defined as 1/86,400 of a mean solar day. The standard second is now defined more precisely in terms of the frequency of radiation emit-

Standard of time (second)

TABLE 1–1
Some typical Lengths or Distances (order of magnitude)

Length (or distance)	Meters (approximate)
Neutron or proton (radius)	10^{-15} m
Atom	10^{-10} m
Virus [see Fig. 1–6]	10^{-7} m
Sheet of paper (thickness)	10^{-4} m
Finger width	10^{-2} m
Football field length	10^{2} m
Mt. Everest height [see Fig. 1–6]	10^{4} m
Earth diameter	10^{7} m
Earth to Sun	10^{11} m
Nearest star, distance	10^{16} m
Nearest galaxy	10^{22} m
Farthest galaxy visible	10^{26} m

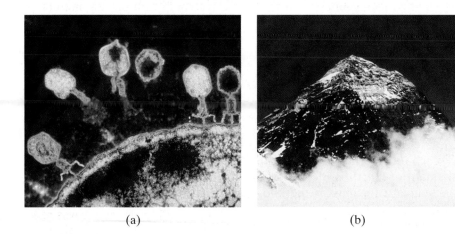

(a)   (b)

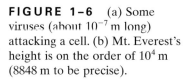

FIGURE 1–6 (a) Some viruses (about 10^{-7} m long) attacking a cell. (b) Mt. Everest's height is on the order of 10^{4} m (8848 m to be precise).

[†]The new definition of the meter has the effect of giving the speed of light the exact value of 299,792,458 m/s.

TABLE 1–2 Some typical Time Intervals	
Time interval	Seconds (approximate)
Lifetime of very unstable particle	10^{-23} s
Lifetime of radioactive elements	10^{-22} s to 10^{28} s
Lifetime of muon	10^{-6} s
Time between human heartbeats	10^{0} s ($=1$ s)
One day	10^{5} s
One year	3×10^{7} s
Human life span	2×10^{9} s
Length of recorded history	10^{11} s
Humans on Earth	10^{14} s
Life on Earth	10^{17} s
Age of Universe	10^{18} s

TABLE 1–3 Some Masses	
Object	Kilograms (approx.)
Electron	10^{-30} kg
Proton, neutron	10^{-27} kg
DNA molecule	10^{-17} kg
Bacterium	10^{-15} kg
Mosquito	10^{-5} kg
Plum	10^{-1} kg
Person	10^{2} kg
Ship	10^{8} kg
Earth	6×10^{24} kg
Sun	2×10^{30} kg
Galaxy	10^{41} kg

ted by cesium atoms when they pass between two particular states. Specifically, one second is defined as the time required for 9,192,631,770 periods of this radiation. There are, of course, precisely 60 s in one minute (min) and 60 minutes in one hour (h). Note that these two factors of 60 (as well as the 2.54 cm per inch) are definitions and hence have an indefinite number of significant figures. Table 1–2 presents a range of measured time intervals.

Standard of mass (kilogram)

The standard unit of **mass** is the **kilogram** (kg). The standard mass is a particular platinum–iridium cylinder, kept at the International Bureau of Weights and Measures near Paris, France, whose mass is defined as exactly 1 kg. A range of masses is presented in Table 1–3. [For practical purposes, 1 kg weighs about 2.2 pounds.]

When dealing with atoms and molecules, the **unified atomic mass unit** (u) is usually used. In terms of the kilogram

$$1 \text{ u} = 1.6605 \times 10^{-27} \text{ kg}.$$

The definitions of other standard units for other quantities will be given as we encounter them in later chapters.

In the metric system, the larger and smaller units are defined in multiples of 10 from the standard unit, and this makes calculation particularly easy. Thus 1 kilometer (km) is 1000 m, 1 centimeter is $\frac{1}{100}$ m, 1 millimeter (mm) is $\frac{1}{1000}$ m or $\frac{1}{10}$ cm, and so on. The prefixes "centi-," "kilo-," and others are listed in Table 1–4 and can be applied not only to units of length, but to units of volume, mass, or any other metric unit. For example, a centiliter (cL) is $\frac{1}{100}$ liter (L) and a kilogram (kg) is 1000 grams (g).

When dealing with the laws and equations of physics it is very important to use a consistent set of units. Several systems of units have been in use over the years. Today the most important is the **Système International** (French for International System), which is abbreviated SI. In SI units, the standard of length is the meter, the standard for time is the second, and the standard for mass is the kilogram. This system used to be called the MKS (meter-kilogram-second) system.

A second metric system is the **cgs system**, in which the centimeter, gram, and second are the standard units of length, mass, and time, as abbreviated in the title. The **British engineering system** takes as its standards the foot for length, the pound for force, and the second for time.

SI units are the principal ones used today in scientific work. We will therefore use SI units almost exclusively in this book, although we will give the cgs and British units for various quantities when introduced.

1-6 Converting Units

Any quantity we measure, such as a length, a speed, or an electric current, consists of a number *and* a unit. Often we are given a quantity in one set of units, but we want it expressed in another set of units. For example, suppose we measure that a table is 21.5 inches wide, and we want to express this in centimeters. We must use a **conversion factor** which in this case is

$$1 \text{ in.} = 2.54 \text{ cm}$$

or, written another way,

$$1 = 2.54 \text{ cm/in.}$$

Since multiplying by one does not change anything, the width of our table, in cm, is

$$21.5 \text{ inches} = (21.5 \text{ in.}) \times \left(2.54 \frac{\text{cm}}{\text{in.}}\right) = 54.6 \text{ cm}$$

Note how the units (inches in this case) cancelled out. A table containing many unit conversions is found inside the front cover of this book. Let's take some Examples.

EXAMPLE 1-2 **The 100-m dash.** What is the length of the 100-m dash expressed in yards?

SOLUTION Let us assume the distance is accurately known to four significant figures, 100.0 m. One yard (yd) is precisely 3 feet (36 inches), so we can write

$$1 \text{ yd} = 3 \text{ ft} = 36 \text{ in.} = (36 \text{ in.}) \left(2.540 \frac{\text{cm}}{\text{in.}}\right) = 91.44 \text{ cm}$$

or,

$$1 \text{ yd} = 0.9144 \text{ m},$$

since $1 \text{ m} = 100 \text{ cm}$. We can rewrite this result as

$$1 \text{ m} = \frac{1 \text{ yd}}{0.9144} = 1.094 \text{ yd}.$$

Then

$$100 \text{ m} = (100 \text{ m}) \left(1.094 \frac{\text{yd}}{\text{m}}\right) = 109.4 \text{ yd},$$

so a 100-m dash is 9.4 yards longer than a 100-yard dash.

TABLE 1-4 Metric (SI) Prefixes		
Prefix	**Abbreviation**	**Value**
exa	E	10^{18}
peta	P	10^{15}
tera	T	10^{12}
giga	G	10^{9}
mega	M	10^{6}
kilo	k	10^{3}
hecto	h	10^{2}
deka	da	10^{1}
deci	d	10^{-1}
centi	c	10^{-2}
milli	m	10^{-3}
micro[†]	μ	10^{-6}
nano	n	10^{-9}
pico	p	10^{-12}
femto	f	10^{-15}
atto	a	10^{-18}

[†] μ is the Greek letter "mu."

EXAMPLE 1–3 **Area of a cell membrane.** A round membrane has an area of 1.25 square inches. Express this in square centimeters.

SOLUTION   Because 1 in. = 2.54 cm, then

$$1 \text{ in.}^2 = (2.54 \text{ cm})^2 = 6.45 \text{ cm}^2.$$

So

$$1.25 \text{ in.}^2 = (1.25 \text{ in.}^2)\left(2.54 \frac{\text{cm}}{\text{in.}}\right)^2 = (1.25 \text{ in.}^2)\left(6.45 \frac{\text{cm}^2}{\text{in.}^2}\right) = 8.06 \text{ cm.}^2$$

EXAMPLE 1–4 **Speeds.** Where the posted speed limit is 55 miles per hour (mi/h or mph), what is this speed (*a*) in meters per second (m/s) and (*b*) in kilometers per hour (km/h)?

SOLUTION   (*a*) We can write 1 mile as

$$1 \text{ mi} = (5280 \text{ ft})\left(12 \frac{\text{in.}}{\text{ft}}\right)\left(2.54 \frac{\text{cm}}{\text{in.}}\right)\left(\frac{1 \text{ m}}{100 \text{ cm}}\right) = 1609 \text{ m}.$$

Note that each conversion factor is equal to one. We also know that 1 hour equals (60 min/h) × (60 s/min) = 3600 s/h, so

$$55 \frac{\text{mi}}{\text{h}} = \left(55 \frac{\text{mi}}{\text{h}}\right)\left(1609 \frac{\text{m}}{\text{mi}}\right)\left(\frac{1 \text{ h}}{3600 \text{ s}}\right) = 25 \text{ m/s}.$$

(*b*) Now we use 1 mi = 1609 m = 1.609 km; then

$$55 \frac{\text{mi}}{\text{h}} = \left(55 \frac{\text{mi}}{\text{h}}\right)\left(1.609 \frac{\text{km}}{\text{mi}}\right) = 88 \frac{\text{km}}{\text{h}}.$$

Conversion factors = 1

When changing units, you can avoid making an error in the use of conversion factors by checking that units cancel out properly. For example, in our conversion of 1 mi to 1609 m in Example 1–4(*a*), if we had incorrectly used the factor $\left(\frac{100 \text{ cm}}{1 \text{ m}}\right)$ instead of $\left(\frac{1 \text{ m}}{100 \text{ cm}}\right)$, the meter units would not have cancelled out; we would not have ended up with meters.

➡ **P R O B L E M   S O L V I N G**

Unit conversion is wrong if units do not cancel

1–7 Order of Magnitude: Rapid Estimating

We are sometimes interested only in an approximate value for a quantity. This might be because an accurate calculation would take more time than it is worth or would require additional data that are not available. In other cases, we may want to make a rough estimate in order to check an accurate calculation made on a calculator, to make sure that no blunders were made when entering the numbers.

A rough estimate is made by rounding off all numbers to one significant figure and its power of 10, and after the calculation is made, again only one significant figure is kept. Such an estimate is called an **order-of-magnitude estimate** and can be accurate within a factor of 10, and often better. In fact, the phrase "order of magnitude" is sometimes used to refer simply to the power of 10.

To give you some idea of how useful and powerful rough estimates can be, let us do a few "worked-out Examples."

➡ **P R O B L E M   S O L V I N G**

How to make a rough estimate

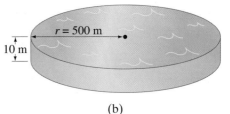

(a)

(b)

FIGURE 1–7 Example 1–5.
(a) How much water is in this lake?
(Photo is of one of the Rae Lakes
in the Sierra Nevada of California.)
(b) Model of the lake as a cylinder.
[We could go one step further and
estimate the mass or weight of this lake.
We will see later that water has a density
of 1000 kg/m^3, so this lake has a mass of
about $(10^3 \text{ kg/m}^3)(10^7 \text{ m}^3) \approx 10^{10} \text{ kg}$,
which is about 10 billion kg or 10 million
metric tons. (A metric ton is 1000 kg,
about 2200 lbs, slightly larger than a
British ton, 2000 lbs.)]

EXAMPLE 1–5 **ESTIMATE** **Volume of a lake.** Estimate how much
water there is in a particular lake, Fig. 1–7, which is roughly circular, about
1 km across, and you guess it to have an average depth of about 10 m.

SOLUTION No lake is a perfect circle, nor can lakes be expected to
have a perfectly flat bottom. We are only estimating here. To estimate the
volume, we use a simple model of the lake as a cylinder: we multiply the
average depth of the lake times its roughly circular surface area, as if the
lake were a cylinder (Fig. 1–7b). The volume V of a cylinder is the product of its height h times the area of its base: $V = h\pi r^2$, where r is the
radius of the circular base. The radius r is $\frac{1}{2}$ km = 500 m, so the volume is
approximately

$$V = h\pi r^2 \approx (10 \text{ m}) \times (3) \times (5 \times 10^2 \text{ m})^2 \approx 8 \times 10^6 \text{ m}^3 \approx 10^7 \text{ m}^3,$$

where π was rounded off to 3; the symbol $\approx$ means "approximately
equal to." So the volume is on the order of 10^7 m^3, ten million cubic
meters. Because of all the estimates that went into this calculation, the
order-of-magnitude estimate (10^7 m^3) is probably better to quote than
the $8 \times 10^6 \text{ m}^3$ figure.

Here's another Example:

FIGURE 1–8 A micrometer,
which is used for measuring small
thicknesses.

EXAMPLE 1–6 **ESTIMATE** **Thickness of a page.** Estimate the thickness of a page of this book.

SOLUTION At first you might think that a special measuring device, a
micrometer (Fig. 1–8), is needed to measure the thickness of one page
since an ordinary ruler clearly won't do. But we can use a trick or, to put

it in physics terms, make use of a *symmetry*: we can make the reasonable assumption that all the pages of this book are equal in thickness. Thus, we can use a ruler to measure hundreds of pages at once. This book is about 1000 pages long, when you count both sides of the page (front and back), so it contains about 500 separate pieces of paper. It is about 4 cm thick (don't include the cover, of course). So if 500 pages are 4 cm thick, one page must be about

$$\frac{4 \text{ cm}}{500 \text{ pages}} \approx 8 \times 10^{-3} \text{ cm} = 8 \times 10^{-2} \text{ mm}$$

or, rounding off even more, about a tenth of a millimeter (0.1 mm), or 10^{-4} m.

Now let's take a simple Example of how a diagram can be useful for making an estimate. It cannot be emphasized enough how important it is to draw a diagram when trying to solve a physics problem.

EXAMPLE 1–7 **ESTIMATE** **Height by triangulation.** Estimate the height of the building shown in Fig. 1–9a, by "triangulation," with the help of a bus-stop pole and a friend.

SOLUTION By standing your friend next to the pole, you estimate the height of the pole to be 3 m. You next step away from the pole until the top of the pole is in line with the top of the building, Fig. 1–9a. You are 5 ft 6 in. tall, so your eyes are about 1.5 m above the ground. Your friend is taller, and when she stretches out her arms, one hand touches you, and the other touches the pole, so you estimate that distance as 2 m (Fig. 1–9a). You then pace off the distance from the pole to the base of the building with big, 1-m-long, steps, and you get a total of 16 steps or 16 m. Now you draw, to scale, the diagram shown in Fig. 1–9b using these measurements. You can measure, right on the diagram, the last side of the triangle to be about $x = 13$ m. Alternatively, you can use similar triangles to obtain the height x:

$$\frac{1.5 \text{ m}}{2 \text{ m}} = \frac{x}{18 \text{ m}}, \qquad \text{so} \quad x \approx 13\tfrac{1}{2} \text{ m.}$$

Finally you add in your eye height of 1.5 m above the ground to get your final result: the building is about 15 m tall.

FIGURE 1–9 Example 1–7. Diagrams are really useful!

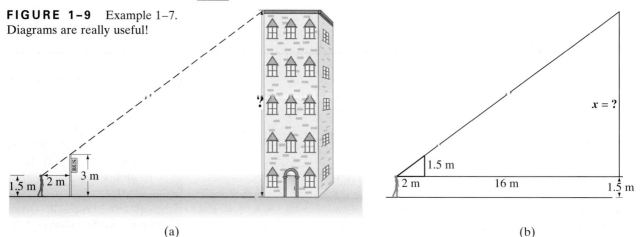

(a)   (b)

Another example, this one made famous by the physicist Enrico Fermi, is to estimate the number of piano tuners in a city, say, Chicago or San Francisco. To get a rough order-of-magnitude estimate of the number of piano tuners today in San Francisco, a city of about 700,000 inhabitants, we can proceed by estimating the number of functioning pianos, how often each piano is tuned, and how many pianos each tuner can tune. To estimate the number of pianos in San Francisco, we note that certainly not everyone has a piano. A guess of 1 family in 5 or 6 having a piano would correspond to 1 piano per 20 persons, assuming an average family of 3 or 4 persons. As an order of magnitude, 1 piano per 20 people is certainly more reasonable than 1 per 100 people, or 1 per every person, so let's proceed with the estimate that 1 person in 20 has a piano, or about 35,000 pianos in San Francisco. Now a piano tuner needs an hour or two to tune a piano. So let's estimate that a tuner can tune about 3 pianos a day. A piano ought to be tuned every 6 months or a year—let's say once each year. A piano tuner tuning 3 pianos a day, 5 days a week, 50 weeks a year can tune about 700 pianos a year. So San Francisco, with its (very) roughly 35,000 pianos needs about 50 piano tuners. This is, of course, only a rough estimate. It tells us that there must be many more than 5 piano tuners, and surely not as many as 500. A check of the San Francisco Yellow Pages (done after this calculation) reveals about 50 listings. Each of these listings may employ more than one tuner, but on the other hand, each may also do repairs as well as tuning. In any case, our estimate is reasonable.

➡ **PROBLEM SOLVING**

Estimating how many piano tuners there are in a city

1–8 Mathematics in Physics

Physics is sometimes thought of as being a difficult subject. However, sometimes it is the mathematics used that is the source of difficulties rather than the physics itself. The appendices at the end of this book contain a brief summary of simple mathematical techniques, including algebra, geometry, and trigonometry, that will be used in this book. You may find it useful to examine those appendices now to review old topics or learn any new ones. You may also want to reread them later when you need those concepts. Some mathematical techniques, such as vectors and trigonometric functions, are treated in the text itself, when we first need them.

Check the mathematical Appendices (end of book)

▌ SUMMARY

[The Summary that appears at the end of each chapter in this book gives a brief overview of the main ideas of the chapter. The Summary *cannot* serve to give an understanding of the material, which can be accomplished only by a detailed reading of the chapter.]

Physics, like other sciences, is a creative endeavor. It is not simply a collection of facts. Important theories are created with the idea of explaining observations. To be accepted, theories are "tested" by comparing their predictions with the results of actual experiments. Note that, in general, a theory cannot be "proved" in an absolute sense.

Scientists often devise models of physical phenomena. A **model** is a kind of picture or analogy that seems to explain the phenomena. A **theory**, often developed from a model, is usually deeper and more complex than a simple model.

A scientific **law** is a concise statement, often expressed in the form of an equation, which quantitatively describes a particular range of phenomena over a wide range of cases.

Measurements play a crucial role in physics, but can never be perfectly precise. It is important to specify the **uncertainty** of a measurement either by stating it directly using the ± notation, and/or by keeping only the correct number of **significant figures**.

Physical quantities are always specified relative to a particular standard or **unit**, and the unit used should always be stated. The commonly accepted set of units today is the **Système International** (SI), in which the standard units of length, mass, and time are the **meter**, **kilogram**, and **second**.

When converting units, check all **conversion factors** for correct cancellation of units.

Making rough, **order-of-magnitude estimates** is a very useful technique in science as well as in everyday life.

◼ QUESTIONS

1. It is advantageous that fundamental standards, such as those for length and time, be accessible (easy to compare to), invariable (do not change), indestructible, and reproducible. Discuss why these are advantages and whether any of these criteria can be incompatible with others.

2. What are the merits and drawbacks of using a person's foot as a standard? Discuss in terms of the criteria mentioned in Question 1. Consider both (*a*) a particular person's foot, and (*b*) any person's foot.

3. When traveling a highway in the mountains, you may see elevation signs that read "914 m (3000 ft)." Critics of the metric system claim that such numbers show the metric system is more complicated. How would you alter such signs to be more consistent with a switch to the metric system?

4. Suggest a way to measure the distance from Earth to the Sun.

5. What is wrong with this road sign:
   Boston 7 mi (11.263 km)?

6. List assumptions useful to estimate the number of car mechanics in (*a*) San Francisco, (*b*) your hometown, and then make the estimates.

7. Discuss how you would estimate the number of hours you have spent in school thus far in your life. Then make the estimate.

8. Discuss how the notion of symmetry could be used to estimate the number of marbles in a one-liter jar.

9. You measure the radius of a wheel to be 4.16 cm. If you multiply by 2 to get the diameter, should you write the result as 8 cm or as 8.32 cm? Justify your answer.

◼ PROBLEMS

[The problems at the end of each chapter are ranked I, II, or III according to estimated difficulty, with I problems being easiest. The problems are arranged by Sections, meaning that the reader should have read up to and including that Section, but not only that Section—problems often depend on earlier material. Each chapter also has a group of General Problems that are not arranged by Section and not ranked.]

SECTION 1–4

1. (I) The age of the universe is thought to be somewhere around 10 billion years. Assuming one significant figure, write this in powers of ten in (*a*) years, (*b*) seconds.

2. (I) Write out the following numbers in full with a decimal point and correct number of zeros: (*a*) 8.69×10^4, (*b*) 7.1×10^3, (*c*) 6.6×10^{-1}, (*d*) 8.76×10^2, and (*e*) 8.62×10^{-5}.

3. (I) Write the following numbers in powers of ten notation: (*a*) 1,156,000, (*b*) 218, (*c*) 0.0068, (*d*) 27.635, (*e*) 0.21, and (*f*) 22.

4. (I) How many significant figures do each of the following numbers have: (*a*) 142, (*b*) 81.60, (*c*) 7.63, (*d*) 0.03, (*e*) 0.0086, (*f*) 3236, and (*g*) 8700?

5. (I) What is the percent uncertainty in the measurement 2.26 ± 0.25 m?

6. (I) What, approximately, is the percent uncertainty for the measurement 1.67?

7. (I) Time intervals measured with a stopwatch typically have an uncertainty of about a half second, due to human reaction time at the start and stop moments. What is the percent uncertainty of a hand-timed measurement of (a) 5 s, (b) 50 s, (c) 5 min?

8. (II) Multiply 2.079×10^2 m by 0.072×10^{-1}, taking into account significant figures.

9. (II) Add 7.2×10^3 s $+ 8.3 \times 10^4$ s $+ 0.09 \times 10^6$ s.

10. (II) What is the area, and its approximate uncertainty, of a circle of radius 2.8×10^4 cm?

11. (II) What is the percent uncertainty in the volume of a spherical beach ball whose radius is $r = 3.86 \pm 0.08$ m?

SECTIONS 1–5 AND 1–6

12. (I) Express the following using the prefixes of Table 1–4: (a) 10^6 volts, (b) 10^{-6} meters, (c) 5×10^3 days, (d) 8×10^2 bucks, and (e) 8×10^{-9} pieces.

13. (I) Write the following as full (decimal) numbers with standard units: (a) 86.6 mm, (b) 35 μV, (c) 860 mg, (d) 600 picoseconds, (e) 12.5 femtometers, (f) 250 gigavolts.

14. (I) How many kisses is 50 hectokisses? What would you be if you earned a megabuck a year?

15. (I) Determine your height in meters.

16. (I) The Sun, on average, is 93 million miles from the Earth. How many meters is this? Express (a) using powers of ten, and (b) using a metric prefix.

17. (II) A typical atom has a diameter of about 1.0×10^{-10} m. (a) What is this in inches? (b) How many atoms are there along a 1.0-cm line?

18. (II) Express the following sum with the correct number of significant figures:

$$1.00 \text{ m} + 142.5 \text{ cm} + 1.24 \times 10^5 \text{ } \mu\text{m}.$$

19. (II) Determine the conversion factor between (a) km/h and mi/h, (b) m/s and ft/s, and (c) km/h and m/s.

20. (II) How much longer (percentage) is a one-mile race than a 1500-m race ("the metric mile")?

21. (II) A *light-year* is the distance light (speed = 2.998×10^8 m/s) travels in 1.00 year. (a) How many meters are there in 1.00 light-year? (b) An astronomical unit (AU) is the average distance from the Sun to Earth, 1.50×10^8 km. How many AU are there in 1.00 light-year? (c) What is the speed of light in AU/h?

22. (III) The diameter of the moon is 3480 km. What is the surface area, and how does it compare to the land surface area of the Earth?

SECTION 1–7

(*Note*: Remember that for rough estimates, only round numbers are needed both as input to calculations and as final results.)

23. (I) Estimate the order of magnitude (power of ten) of: (a) 7800, (b) 9.630×10^2, (c) 0.00076, and (d) 150×10^8.

24. (II) Estimate how long it would take a good runner to run across the United States from New York to California.

25. (II) Make a rough estimate of the percentage of a house's outside wall area that consists of window area.

26. (II) Estimate the number of times a human heart beats in a lifetime.

27. (II) Make a rough estimate of the volume of your body (in cm^3).

28. (II) Estimate the time to drive from Beijing (Peking) to Paris (a) today, and (b) in 1906 when a great car race was run between those two cities.

29. (II) Estimate the number of dentists (a) in San Francisco and (b) in your town or city.

30. (II) Estimate how long it would take one person to mow a football field using an ordinary home lawn mower.

31. (III) The rubber worn from tires mostly enters the atmosphere as particulate pollution. Estimate how much rubber (in kg) is put into the air in the United States every year. To get you started, a good estimate for a tire tread's depth is 1 cm when new, and the density of rubber is about 1200 kg/m^3.

▮ GENERAL PROBLEMS

32. An angstrom (symbol Å) is an older unit of length, defined as 10^{-10} m. (a) How many nanometers are in 1.0 angstrom? (b) How many femtometers (the common unit of length in nuclear physics) are in 1.0 angstrom? (c) How many angstroms are in 1.0 meter? (d) How many angstroms are in 1.0 light-year (see Problem 21)?

33. (a) How many seconds are there in 1.00 year? (b) How many nanoseconds are there in 1.00 year? (c) How many years are there in 1.00 second?

34. Estimate the number of bus drivers (a) in Washington, D.C., and (b) in your town.

FIGURE 1–10 Problem 35. The wafer held by hand (above) is shown below, enlarged and illuminated by colored light. Visible are rows of integrated circuits (chips).

35. Computer chips (Fig. 1–10) are etched on circular silicon wafers of thickness 0.60 mm that are sliced from a solid cylindrical silicon crystal of length 30 cm. If each wafer can hold 100 chips, what is the maximum number of chips that can be produced from one entire cylinder?

36. Estimate the number of gallons of gasoline consumed by automobile drivers in the United States, per year.

37. Estimate the number of gumballs in the machine shown in Fig. 1–11.

FIGURE 1–11 Problem 37. Estimate the number of gumballs in the machine.

38. An average family of four uses roughly 1200 liters (about 300 gallons) of water per day. (One liter = 1000 cm³.) How much depth would a lake lose per year if it uniformly covered an area of 50 square kilometers and supplied a local town with a population of 40,000 people? Consider only population uses, and neglect evaporation and so on.

39. How big is a ton? That is, what is the volume of something that weighs a ton? To be specific, estimate the diameter of a 1-ton rock, but first make a wild guess: will it be 1 ft across, 3 ft, or the size of a car? [*Hint:* Rock has mass per volume about 3 times that of water, which is 1 kg per liter (10^3 cm³) or 62 lbs per cubic foot.]

40. A violent rainstorm dumps 1.0 cm of rain on a city 5 km wide and 8 km long in a 2-h period. How many metric tons (1 ton = 10^3 kg) of water fell on the city? [1 cm³ of water has a mass of 1 gram = 10^{-3} kg.]

41. Hold a pencil in front of your eye at a position where its end just blocks out the Moon (Fig. 1–12). Make appropriate measurements to estimate the diameter of the Moon, given that the Earth–Moon distance is 3.8×10^5 km.

42. The volume of an object is 1000 m³. Express this volume in (*a*) cm³, (*b*) ft³, (*c*) in.³.

43. Estimate how long it would take to walk around the world.

44. Noah's ark was ordered to be 300 cubits long, 50 cubits wide, and 30 cubits high. The cubit was a unit of measure equal to the length of a human forearm, elbow to the tip of the longest finger. Express the dimensions of Noah's ark in meters.

FIGURE 1–12 Problem 41. How big is the Moon?

Space shuttle Discovery landing on Earth. The parachute helps it to reduce its speed quickly. The directions of Discovery's velocity and acceleration are shown by the green (**v**) and gold (**a**) arrows. Note that they (**v** and **a**) point in opposite directions.

DESCRIBING MOTION: KINEMATICS IN ONE DIMENSION

The motion of objects—baseballs, automobiles, joggers, and even the Sun and Moon—is an obvious part of everyday life. Although the ancients acquired significant insight into motion, it was not until comparatively recently, in the sixteenth and seventeenth centuries, that our modern understanding of motion was established. Many contributed to this understanding, but, as we shall soon see, two individuals stand out above the rest: Galileo Galilei (1564–1642) and Isaac Newton (1642–1727).

The study of the motion of objects, and the related concepts of force and energy, form the field called **mechanics**. Mechanics is customarily divided into two parts: **kinematics**, which is the description of how objects move, and **dynamics**, which deals with force and why objects move as they do. This chapter and the next deal with kinematics.

We start by discussing objects that move without rotating (Fig. 2–1a). Such motion is called **translational motion**. In the present chapter we will be concerned with describing an object that moves along a straight-line path, which is one-dimensional motion. In Chapter 3 we will study how to describe translational motion in two (or three) dimensions.

(a)   (b)

FIGURE 2–1 The pinecone in (a) undergoes pure translation as it falls, whereas in (b) it is rotating as well as translating.

19

All measurements are made relative to a frame of reference

Any measurement of position, distance, or speed must be made with respect to a **frame of reference**. For example, while you are on a train traveling at 80 km/h, you might notice a person who walks past you toward the front of the train at a speed of, say, 5 km/h (Fig. 2–2). Of course this is the person's speed with respect to the train as frame of reference. With respect to the ground that person is moving at a speed of 80 km/h + 5 km/h = 85 km/h. It is always important to specify the frame of reference when stating a speed. In everyday life, we usually mean "with respect to the Earth" without even thinking about it, but the reference frame should be specified whenever there might be confusion.

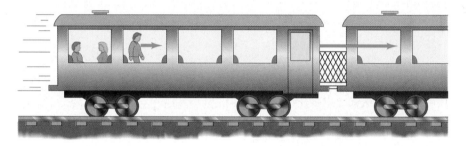

FIGURE 2–2 A person walks toward the front of a train at 5 km/h. The train is moving 80 km/h with respect to the ground, so the walking person's speed, relative to the ground, is 85 km/h.

When specifying the motion of an object, it is important to specify not only the speed but also the direction of motion. Often we can specify a direction by using the cardinal points, north, east, south, and west, and by "up" and "down." In physics, we often draw a set of **coordinate axes**, as shown in Fig. 2–3, to represent a frame of reference. We can always place the origin 0, and the directions of the *x* and *y* axes, as we like for convenience. Objects positioned to the right of the origin of coordinates (0) on the *x* axis have an *x* coordinate which we usually choose to be positive; then points to the left of 0 have a negative *x* coordinate. The position along the *y* axis is usually considered positive when above 0, and negative when below 0, although the reverse convention can be used if convenient. Any point on the plane can be specified by giving its *x* and *y* coordinates. In three dimensions, a *z* axis perpendicular to the *x* and *y* axes is also used.

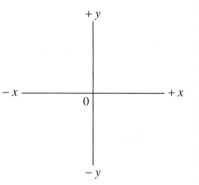

FIGURE 2–3 Standard set of *xy* coordinate axes.

For one-dimensional motion, we often choose the *x* axis as the line along which the motion takes place. Thus the position of an object at any moment is given by its *x* coordinate.

Displacement

We need to make a distinction between the distance an object has traveled, and its **displacement**, which is defined as the *change in position* of the object. That is, displacement is how far the object is from its starting point. To see the distinction between total distance and displacement, imagine a person walking 70 m to the east and then turning around and walking back (west) a distance of 30 m (see Fig. 2–4). The total *distance* traveled is 100 m, but the *displacement* is only 40 m since the person is now only 40 m from the starting point.

Displacement is a quantity that has both magnitude and direction. Such quantities are called **vectors**, and are represented in diagrams by arrows. For example, in Fig. 2–4, the blue arrow represents the displacement whose magnitude is 40 m and whose direction is to the right.

We will deal with vectors more fully in Chapter 3. For now, we deal only with motion in one dimension, along a line, and in this case, vectors which point in one direction will have a positive sign, whereas vectors that point in the opposite direction will have a negative sign.

Let's see how this works. Consider the motion of an object over a particular time interval. Suppose that at some initial moment in time, call it t_1, the object is on the x axis at the point x_1 in the coordinate system shown in Fig. 2–5. At some later time, t_2, suppose the object is at point x_2. The displacement of our object is $x_2 - x_1$, and is represented by the arrow pointing to the right in Fig. 2–5. It is convenient to write

$$\Delta x = x_2 - x_1$$

where the symbol Δ (Greek letter delta) means "change in." Then Δx means "the change in x," which is the displacement. Note that the "change in" any quantity means the final value of that quantity minus the initial value.

To be concrete, suppose $x_1 = 10.0$ m and $x_2 = 30.0$ m. Then

$$\Delta x = x_2 - x_1 = 30.0 \text{ m} - 10.0 \text{ m} = 20.0 \text{ m}.$$

See Fig. 2–5.

Now consider a different situation, that of an object moving to the left as shown in Fig. 2–6. Here an object, say a person, starts at $x_1 = 30.0$ m and walks to the left to the point $x_2 = 10.0$ m. In this case

$$\Delta x = x_2 - x_1 = 10.0 \text{ m} - 30.0 \text{ m} = -20.0 \text{ m}$$

and the blue arrow representing the vector displacement points to the left. This example illustrates that when dealing with one-dimensional motion, a vector pointing to the right has a positive value, whereas one pointing to the left has a negative value.

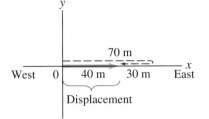

FIGURE 2–4 A person walks 70 m east, then 30 m west. The total distance traveled is 100 m (path is shown in black); but the displacement, shown as a blue arrow, is 40 m to the east.

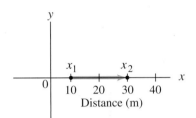

FIGURE 2–5 The arrow represents the displacement $x_2 - x_1$. Distances are in meters.

FIGURE 2–6 For the displacement $\Delta x = x_2 - x_1 = 10.0$ m $- 30.0$ m, the displacement vector points to the left.

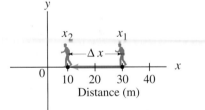

2–2 Average Velocity

The most obvious aspect of the motion of a moving object is how fast it is moving—its speed or velocity.

The term "speed" refers to how far an object travels in a given time interval. If a car travels 240 kilometers (km) in 3 hours, we say its average speed was 80 km/h. In general, the **average speed** of an object is defined as *the distance traveled along its path divided by the time it takes to travel this distance:*

$$\text{average speed} = \frac{\text{distance traveled}}{\text{time elapsed}}. \qquad (2–1)$$ *Average speed*

The terms velocity and speed are often used interchangeably in ordinary language. But in physics we make a distinction between the two. Speed is simply a positive number, with units. **Velocity**, on the other hand, is used to signify both the *magnitude* (numerical value) of how fast an object is moving and the *direction* in which it is moving. (Velocity is therefore a vector.) There *Velocity* is a second difference between speed and velocity: namely, the **average velocity** is defined in terms of *displacement*, rather than total distance traveled:

$$\text{average velocity} = \frac{\text{displacement}}{\text{time elapsed}}.$$

Average speed and average velocity often have the same magnitude, but sometimes they don't. As an example, recall the walk we described earlier, in Fig. 2–4, where a person walked 70 m east and then 30 m west. The total distance traveled was 70 m + 30 m = 100 m, but the displacement was 40 m. Suppose this walk took 70 s to complete. Then the average speed was:

$$\frac{\text{distance}}{\text{time}} = \frac{100 \text{ m}}{70 \text{ s}} = 1.4 \text{ m/s}.$$

The magnitude of the average velocity, on the other hand, was:

$$\frac{\text{displacement}}{\text{time}} = \frac{40 \text{ m}}{70 \text{ s}} = 0.57 \text{ m/s}.$$

This discrepancy between the speed and the magnitude of the velocity occurs in some cases, but only for the *average* values, and we rarely need be concerned with it.

To discuss one-dimensional motion of an object in general, suppose that at some moment in time, call it t_1, the object is on the x axis at point x_1 in a coordinate system, and at some later time, t_2, suppose it is at point x_2. The elapsed time is $t_2 - t_1$, and during this time interval the displacement of our object was $\Delta x = x_2 - x_1$. Then the average velocity, defined as *the displacement divided by the elapsed time*, can be written

Average velocity

$$\bar{v} = \frac{x_2 - x_1}{t_2 - t_1} = \frac{\Delta x}{\Delta t}, \tag{2–2}$$

where v stands for velocity and the bar ($^{-}$) over the v is a standard symbol meaning "average."

Notice that if x_2 is less than x_1, the object is moving to the left, and then $\Delta x = x_2 - x_1$ is less than zero. The sign of the displacement, and thus of the velocity, indicates the direction: the average velocity is positive for an object moving to the right along the x axis and negative when the object moves to the left. The direction of the velocity is always the same as the direction of the displacement.

EXAMPLE 2–1   Runner's average velocity. The position of a runner as a function of time is plotted as moving along the x axis of a coordinate system. During a 3.00-s time interval, the runner's position changes from $x_1 = 50.0$ m to $x_2 = 30.5$ m, as shown in Fig. 2–7. What was the runner's average velocity?

SOLUTION Average velocity is the displacement divided by the elapsed time. The displacement is $\Delta x = x_2 - x_1 = 30.5 \text{ m} - 50.0 \text{ m} = -19.5 \text{ m}$. The time interval is $\Delta t = 3.00$ s. Therefore the average velocity is

$$\bar{v} = \frac{\Delta x}{\Delta t} = \frac{-19.5 \text{ m}}{3.00 \text{ s}} = -6.50 \text{ m/s}.$$

The displacement and average velocity are negative, which tells us (if we didn't already know it) that the runner is moving to the left along the x axis, as indicated by the arrow in Fig. 2–7. Thus we can say that the runner's average velocity was 6.50 m/s to the left.

FIGURE 2–7   Example 2–1. A person runs from $x_1 = 50.0$ m to $x_2 = 30.5$ m. The displacement is − 19.5 m.

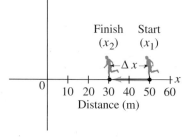

22

EXAMPLE 2–2 **Distance a cyclist travels.** How far can a cyclist travel in 2.5 h along a straight road if her average speed is 18 km/h?

SOLUTION We want to find the distance traveled, so we use Eq. 2–2 letting Δx be the distance and $\overline{v}$ be the average speed, and then rewrite it as

$$\Delta x = \overline{v} \, \Delta t = (18 \text{ km/h})(2.5 \text{ h}) = 45 \text{ km}.$$

2–3 Instantaneous Velocity

If you drive a car along a straight road for 150 km in 2.0 h, the magnitude of your average velocity is 75 km/h. It is unlikely, though, that you were moving at precisely 75 km/h at every instant. To deal with this situation we need the concept of *instantaneous velocity*, which is the velocity at any instant of time. (This is the magnitude that a speedometer is supposed to indicate.) More precisely, the **instantaneous velocity** at any moment is defined as *the average velocity over an infinitesimally short time interval.* That is, starting with Eq. 2–2

$$\overline{v} = \frac{\Delta x}{\Delta t},$$

we define instantaneous velocity as the average velocity in the limit of Δt becoming extremely small, approaching zero. We can write the definition of instantaneous velocity, v, for one-dimensional motion as

$$v = \lim_{\Delta t \to 0} \frac{\Delta x}{\Delta t}. \qquad\qquad \textbf{(2–3)} \quad \textit{Instantaneous velocity}$$

The notation $\lim_{\Delta t \to 0}$ means the ratio $\Delta x/\Delta t$ is to be evaluated in the limit of Δt approaching zero. But we do not simply set $\Delta t = 0$ in this definition, for then Δx would also be zero, and we would have an undefined number. Rather, we are considering the ratio $\Delta x/\Delta t$ as a whole. As we let Δt approach zero, Δx approaches zero as well. But the ratio $\Delta x/\Delta t$ approaches some definite value, which is the instantaneous velocity at a given instant.[†]

For instantaneous velocity we use the symbol v, whereas for average velocity we use $\overline{v}$, with a bar. In the rest of this book, when we use the term "velocity" it will refer to instantaneous velocity. When we want to speak of the average velocity, we will make this clear by including the word "average." Note that the *instantaneous* speed always equals the magnitude of the instantaneous velocity. Why? Because distance and displacement become the same when they become infinitesimally small.

If an object moves at a uniform (that is, constant) velocity over a particular time interval, then its instantaneous velocity at any instant is the same as its average velocity (see Fig. 2–8a). But in many situations this is not the case. For example, a car may start from rest, speed up to 50 km/h, remain at that velocity for a time, then slow down to 20 km/h in a traffic jam, and finally stop at its destination after traveling a total of 15 km in 30 min. This trip is plotted on the graph of Fig. 2–8b. Also shown on the graph is the average velocity (dashed line), which is $\overline{v} = \Delta x/\Delta t = 15 \text{ km}/0.50 \text{ h} = 30 \text{ km/h}$.

[†]More on this in Section 2–8.

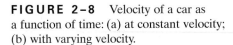

FIGURE 2–8 Velocity of a car as a function of time: (a) at constant velocity; (b) with varying velocity.

2–4 Acceleration

An object whose velocity is changing is said to be accelerating. A car whose velocity increases in magnitude from zero to 80 km/h is accelerating. If one car can accomplish this change in velocity in less time than another, it is said to undergo a greater acceleration. That is, acceleration specifies how rapidly the velocity of an object is changing. **Average acceleration** is defined as the change in velocity divided by the time taken to make this change:

$$\text{average acceleration} = \frac{\text{change of velocity}}{\text{time elapsed}}.$$

In symbols, the average acceleration, $\bar{a}$, over a time interval $\Delta t = t_2 - t_1$ during which the velocity changes by $\Delta v = v_2 - v_1$, is defined as

Average acceleration
$$\bar{a} = \frac{v_2 - v_1}{t_2 - t_1} = \frac{\Delta v}{\Delta t}. \qquad (2\text{–}4)$$

Acceleration is also a vector, but for one-dimensional motion, we need only use a plus or minus sign to indicate direction relative to a chosen coordinate system.

The **instantaneous acceleration**, a, can be defined in analogy to instantaneous velocity, for any specific instant:

Instantaneous acceleration
$$a = \lim_{\Delta t \to 0} \frac{\Delta v}{\Delta t}. \qquad (2\text{–}5)$$

Here Δv represents the very small change in velocity during the very short time interval Δt.

EXAMPLE 2–3 **Average acceleration.** A car accelerates along a straight road from rest to 75 km/h in 5.0 s, Fig. 2–9. What is the magnitude of its average acceleration?

SOLUTION The car starts from rest, so $v_1 = 0$. The final velocity is $v_2 = 75$ km/h. Then from Eq. 2–4, the average acceleration is

$$\bar{a} = \frac{75 \text{ km/h} - 0 \text{ km/h}}{5.0 \text{ s}} = 15 \frac{\text{km/h}}{\text{s}}.$$

This is read as "fifteen kilometers per hour per second" and means that, on average, the velocity changed by 15 km/h during each second. That is, assuming the acceleration was constant, during the first second the car's velocity increased from zero to 15 km/h. During the next second its velocity increased by another 15 km/h up to 30 km/h, and so on, Fig. 2–9. (Of course, if the instantaneous acceleration was not constant, these numbers could be different.)

Careful:
Do not confuse
velocity with acceleration

Note carefully that *acceleration tells us how fast the velocity changes,* whereas *velocity tells us how fast the position changes.* In this last Example, the calculated acceleration contained two different time units: hours and seconds. We

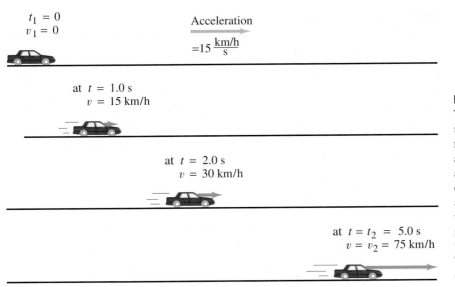

$t_1 = 0$
$v_1 = 0$

Acceleration
$= 15 \dfrac{\text{km/h}}{\text{s}}$

at $t = 1.0$ s
$v = 15$ km/h

at $t = 2.0$ s
$v = 30$ km/h

at $t = t_2 = 5.0$ s
$v = v_2 = 75$ km/h

FIGURE 2–9 Example 2–3. The car is shown at the start with $v_1 = 0$ at $t_1 = 0$. It is shown three more times, at $t = 1.0$ s, $t = 2.0$ s, and $t_2 = 5.0$ s. We assume the acceleration is constant and equals 15 km/h/s. The green arrows represent the velocity vectors; the length of each represents the magnitude of the velocity at that moment. The acceleration vector is the orange arrow.

usually prefer to use only seconds. To do so we can change km/h to m/s (see Section 1–6, and Example 1–4):

$$75 \text{ km/h} = \left(75 \, \frac{\text{km}}{\text{h}}\right)\left(\frac{1000 \text{ m}}{1 \text{ km}}\right)\left(\frac{1 \text{ h}}{3600 \text{ s}}\right) = 21 \text{ m/s}.$$

Then we get

$$\bar{a} = \frac{21 \text{ m/s} - 0.0 \text{ m/s}}{5.0 \text{ s}} = 4.2 \, \frac{\text{m/s}}{\text{s}} = 4.2 \, \frac{\text{m}}{\text{s}^2}.$$

We almost always write these units as m/s² (meters per second squared), as done here, instead of m/s/s. This is possible because:

$$\frac{\text{m/s}}{\text{s}} = \frac{\text{m}}{\text{s} \cdot \text{s}} = \frac{\text{m}}{\text{s}^2}.$$

According to the above calculation, the velocity in Example 2–3 (Fig. 2–9) changed on the average by 4.2 m/s during each second, for a total change of 21 m/s over the 5.0 s.

CONCEPTUAL EXAMPLE 2–4 **Velocity and acceleration.** (*a*) If the velocity of an object is zero, does it mean that the acceleration is zero? (*b*) If the acceleration is zero, does it mean that the velocity is zero? Think of some examples.

RESPONSE A zero velocity does not necessarily mean that the acceleration is zero, nor does a zero acceleration mean that the velocity is zero. (*a*) For example, when you put your foot on the gas pedal of your car which is at rest, the velocity starts from zero but the acceleration is not zero since the velocity of the car changes. (How else could your car start forward if its velocity weren't changing—that is, if the acceleration were zero?) (*b*) As you cruise along a straight highway at a constant velocity of 100 km/h, your acceleration is zero.

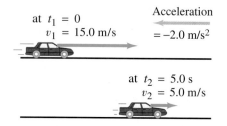

at $t_1 = 0$
$v_1 = 15.0 \text{ m/s}$

Acceleration
$= -2.0 \text{ m/s}^2$

at $t_2 = 5.0 \text{ s}$
$v_2 = 5.0 \text{ m/s}$

FIGURE 2–10 Example 2–5, showing the position of the car at times t_1 and t_2, as well as the car's velocity represented by the green arrows. The acceleration vector (orange) points to the left.

FIGURE 2–11 The same car as in Example 2–5, but now moving to the left and decelerating. The acceleration is

$$a = \frac{v_2 - v_1}{\Delta t} = \frac{-5.0 \text{ m/s} - (-15.0 \text{ m/s})}{5.0 \text{ s}}$$

$$= \frac{-5.0 \text{ m/s} + 15.0 \text{ m/s}}{5.0 \text{ s}} = +2.0 \text{ m/s}^2$$

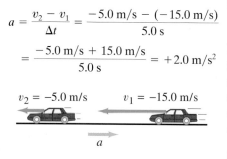

$v_2 = -5.0 \text{ m/s}$ $v_1 = -15.0 \text{ m/s}$

a

EXAMPLE 2–5 **Car slowing down.** An automobile is moving to the right along a straight highway, which we choose to be the positive x axis (Fig. 2–10), and the driver puts on the brakes. If the initial velocity is $v_1 = 15.0 \text{ m/s}$ and it takes 5.0 s to slow down to $v_2 = 5.0 \text{ m/s}$, what was the car's average acceleration?

SOLUTION The average acceleration is equal to the change in velocity divided by the elapsed time, Eq. 2–4. Let us call the initial time $t_1 = 0$; then $t_2 = 5.0 \text{ s}$. (Note that our choice of $t_1 = 0$ doesn't affect the calculation of $\bar{a}$ because only $\Delta t = t_2 - t_1$ appears in Eq. 2–4.) Then

$$\bar{a} = \frac{5.0 \text{ m/s} - 15.0 \text{ m/s}}{5.0 \text{ s}} = -2.0 \text{ m/s}^2.$$

The negative sign appears because the final velocity is less than the initial velocity. In this case the direction of the acceleration is to the left (in the negative x direction)—even though the velocity is always pointing to the right. We say that the acceleration is 2.0 m/s² to the left, and it is shown in Fig. 2–10 as an orange arrow.

When an object is slowing down, we sometimes say it is decelerating. But be careful: deceleration does *not* mean that the acceleration is necessarily negative. For an object moving to the right along the positive x axis and slowing down (as in Fig. 2–10), the acceleration *is* negative. But the same car moving to the left (decreasing x) and slowing down has positive acceleration that points to the right, as shown in Fig. 2–11. We have a deceleration whenever the velocity and acceleration point in opposite directions.

2–5 Motion at Constant Acceleration

Many practical situations occur in which the acceleration is constant or close enough that we can assume it is constant. That is, the acceleration doesn't change over time. We now treat this situation when the magnitude of the acceleration is constant and the motion is in a straight line (sometimes called **uniformly accelerated motion**). In this case, the instantaneous and average accelerations are equal.

To simplify our notation, let us take the initial time in any discussion to be zero: $t_1 = 0$. We can then let $t_2 = t$ be the elapsed time. The initial position (x_1) and initial velocity (v_1) of an object will now be represented by x_0 and v_0; and at time t the position and velocity will be called x and v (rather than x_2 and v_2). The average velocity during the time t will be (from Eq. 2–2)

$$v = \frac{x - x_0}{t - t_0} = \frac{x - x_0}{t}$$

since $t_0 = 0$. And the acceleration, which is assumed constant in time, will be (from Eq. 2–4)

$$a = \frac{v - v_0}{t}.$$

A common problem is to determine the velocity of an object after a certain time, given its acceleration. We can solve such problems by solving

Let a = constant

$t_1 = 0, t_2 = t$
$x_1 = x_0, x_2 = x$
$v_1 = v_0, v_2 = v$

for v in the last equation: we multiply both sides by t and get

$$at = v - v_0$$

and then add v_0 to both sides to obtain:

$$v = v_0 + at. \qquad \text{[constant acceleration]} \quad \textbf{(2-6)}$$

v related to a and t
(a = constant)

For example, it may be known that the acceleration of a particular motorcycle is 4.0 m/s^2, and we wish to determine how fast it will be going after, say, 6.0 s. Assuming it starts from rest ($v_0 = 0$), after 6.0 s the velocity will be $v = at = (4.0 \text{ m/s}^2)(6.0 \text{ s}) = 24 \text{ m/s}$.

Next, let us see how to calculate the position of an object after a time t when it is undergoing constant acceleration. The definition of average velocity (Eq. 2–2) is

$$\bar{v} = \frac{x - x_0}{t},$$

which we can rewrite (solving for x) as

$$x = x_0 + \bar{v}t.$$

Because the velocity increases at a uniform rate, the average velocity, $\bar{v}$, will be midway between the initial and final velocities:

$$\bar{v} = \frac{v_0 + v}{2}. \qquad \text{[constant acceleration]} \quad \textbf{(2-7)}$$

Average velocity
(when acceleration is constant)

(Careful: this is not usually valid if the acceleration is not constant.) We combine the last two equations with Eq. 2–6 and find

$$x = x_0 + \bar{v}t = x_0 + \left(\frac{v_0 + v}{2}\right)t$$

$$= x_0 + \left(\frac{v_0 + v_0 + at}{2}\right)t$$

or

$$x = x_0 + v_0 t + \tfrac{1}{2}at^2. \qquad \text{[constant acceleration]} \quad \textbf{(2-8)}$$

x related to a and t
(a = constant)

Equations 2–6, 2–7, and 2–8 are three of the four most useful equations for motion at constant acceleration. We now derive the fourth equation, which is useful in situations where the time t is not known. We begin as above, with Eq. 2–7 and the equation just before it:

$$x = x_0 + \bar{v}t = x_0 + \left(\frac{v + v_0}{2}\right)t$$

Next we solve Eq. 2–6 for t, obtaining

$$t = \frac{v - v_0}{a},$$

and substituting this into the equation above we have

$$x = x_0 + \left(\frac{v + v_0}{2}\right)\left(\frac{v - v_0}{a}\right) = x_0 + \frac{v^2 - v_0^2}{2a}.$$

We solve this for v^2 and obtain

$$v^2 = v_0^2 + 2a(x - x_0), \qquad \text{[constant acceleration]} \quad \textbf{(2-9)}$$

v related to a and x
(a = constant)

which is the useful equation we sought.

We now have four equations relating position, velocity, acceleration, and time, when the acceleration a is constant. We collect them here in one place for further reference (the tan background screen is to emphasize their usefulness):

Kinematic equations

for constant acceleration

(we'll use them a lot)

$$v = v_0 + at \qquad [a = \text{constant}] \quad \textbf{(2–10a)}$$

$$x = x_0 + v_0 t + \tfrac{1}{2} at^2 \qquad [a = \text{constant}] \quad \textbf{(2–10b)}$$

$$v^2 = v_0^2 + 2a(x - x_0) \qquad [a = \text{constant}] \quad \textbf{(2–10c)}$$

$$\bar{v} = \frac{v + v_0}{2}. \qquad [a = \text{constant}] \quad \textbf{(2–10d)}$$

These useful equations are not valid unless a is a constant. In many cases we can set $x_0 = 0$, and this simplifies the above equations a bit. Note that x represents position, not distance, and $x - x_0$ is the displacement.

EXAMPLE 2–6 **Runway design.** You are designing an airport for small planes. One kind of airplane that might use this airfield must reach a speed before takeoff of at least 27.8 m/s (100 km/h), and can accelerate at 2.00 m/s². (*a*) If the runway is 150 m long, can this airplane reach the proper speed to take off? (*b*) If not, what minimum length must the runway have?

SOLUTION (*a*) We are given the airplane's acceleration ($a = 2.00$ m/s²), and we know the plane can travel a distance of 150 m. We want to find its velocity, to determine if it will be at least 27.8 m/s. We want to find v when we are given:

Known	Wanted
$x_0 = 0$	v
$v_0 = 0$	
$x = 150$ m	
$a = 2.00$ m/s²	

➡ **PROBLEM SOLVING**

Equations 2–10 are valid only when the acceleration is constant, which we assume in this Example

Of the above four equations, Eq. 2–10c will give us v, when we know v_0, a, x, and x_0:

$$v^2 = v_0^2 + 2a(x - x_0)$$

$$= 0 + 2(2.0 \text{ m/s}^2)(150 \text{ m}) = 600 \text{ m}^2/\text{s}^2$$

$$v = \sqrt{600 \text{ m}^2/\text{s}^2} = 24.5 \text{ m/s}.$$

This runway length is *not* sufficient.

(*b*) Now we want $(x - x_0)$ given $v = 27.8$ m/s and $a = 2.0$ m/s². So we use Eq. 2–10c, rewritten as

$$(x - x_0) = \frac{v^2 - v_0^2}{2a} = \frac{(27.8 \text{ m/s})^2 - 0}{2(2.0 \text{ m/s}^2)} = 193 \text{ m}.$$

2–6 Solving Problems

The solving of problems, such as the Examples we have already given, serves two purposes. First, solving problems is useful and practical in itself. Second, solving problems makes you think about the ideas and concepts, and applying the concepts helps you to understand them. But knowing how to do a problem—even to begin it—may not always seem easy. First, it is most important to read the problem through carefully, and more than once. Spend a moment thinking and trying to understand what physics principles, ideas, laws, and definitions might be involved. Up to this point in the book, we have been concerned mainly with the definitions of velocity and acceleration, and the "kinematic equations for constant acceleration," Eqs. 2–10, that we derived from those definitions. For now it is important to note that physics is *not* a collection of equations to be memorized. (In fact, rather than memorizing the very useful Eqs. 2–10, it is better to understand how to derive them from the definitions of velocity and acceleration as we did above.) Simply searching for an equation that might work can be disastrous and can lead you to a wrong result (and will surely not help you understand physics). A better approach is to use the following (rough) procedure, which we put in a special "box" (other such Problem Solving boxes, as an aid, will be found throughout the book):

➡ PROBLEM SOLVING

1. **Read** *and reread* the whole problem carefully before trying to solve it.

2. **Draw** a **diagram** or picture of the situation, with coordinate axes wherever applicable. [You can choose to place the origin of coordinates and the axes wherever you like, so as to make your calculations easier. You also choose which direction is positive and which is negative. Usually we choose the x axis to the right as positive, but you could choose positive to the left.]

3. **Write down** what quantities are "known" or "given," and then what you *want* to know.

4. Think about which principles of physics apply in this problem.

5. Consider which equations (and/or definitions) relate the quantities involved. Before using them, be sure their **range of validity** includes your problem (for example, Eqs. 2–10 are valid only when the acceleration is constant). If you find an applicable equation that involves only known quantities and one desired unknown, **solve** the equation algebraically for the unknown. In many instances several sequential calculations, or a combination of equations, may be needed. It is often preferable to solve algebraically for the desired unknown before putting in numerical values.

6. Carry out the **calculation** if it is a numerical problem. Keep one or two extra digits during the calculations, but round off the final answers to the correct number of significant figures (Section 1–4).

7. Think carefully about the result you obtain: Is it **reasonable**? Does it make sense according to your own intuition and experience? A good check is to do a rough **estimate** using only powers of ten, as discussed in Section 1–7. Often it is preferable to do a rough estimate at the *start* of a numerical problem because it can help you focus your attention on finding a path toward a solution.

8. A very important aspect of doing problems is keeping track of **units**. Note that an equals sign implies the units on each side must be the same, just as the numbers must. If the units do not balance, a mistake has no doubt been made. This can serve as a **check** on your solution (but it only tells you if you're wrong, not if you're right). And: always use a consistent set of units.

➡ **PROBLEM SOLVING**

Note that "starting from rest"
means $v = 0$ at $t = 0$ [i.e., $v_0 = 0$]

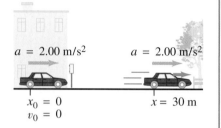

$a = 2.00$ m/s² $a = 2.00$ m/s²

$x_0 = 0$ $x = 30$ m
$v_0 = 0$

FIGURE 2–12   Example 2–7.

➡ **PROBLEM SOLVING**

Check your answer

➡ **PHYSICS APPLIED**

Braking distances

EXAMPLE 2–7   **Acceleration of car.** How long does it take a car to cross a 30.0-m-wide intersection after the light turns green, if it accelerates from rest at a constant 2.00 m/s²?

SOLUTION First we make a sketch, Fig. 2–12. Next we make a table, choosing $x_0 = 0$ and assume the car moves to the right along the positive x axis, and noting that "starting from rest" means $v = 0$ at $t = 0$ [i.e., $v_0 = 0$].

Known	Wanted
$x_0 = 0$	t
$x = 30.0$ m	
$a = 2.00$ m/s²	
$v_0 = 0$	

Since a is constant, we can use Eqs. 2–10. Equation 2–10b is perfect since the only unknown quantity is t. Setting $v_0 = 0$ and $x_0 = 0$, we can solve Eq. 2–10b for t:

$$x = \frac{1}{2} at^2$$

$$t^2 = \frac{2x}{a}$$

$$t = \sqrt{\frac{2x}{a}} = \sqrt{\frac{2(30.0 \text{ m})}{2.00 \text{ m/s}^2}} = 5.48 \text{ s.}$$

This is our answer. Note that the units come out correctly. We can check the reasonableness of the answer by calculating the final velocity $v = at = (2.00 \text{ m/s}^2)(5.48 \text{ s}) = 10.96$ m/s, and then finding $x = x_0 + \bar{v}t = 0 + \frac{1}{2}(10.96 \text{ m/s} + 0)(5.48 \text{ s}) = 30.0$ m, which is our given distance.

EXAMPLE 2–8   **ESTIMATE**   **Braking distances.** Estimate the minimum stopping distances for a car, which are important for traffic safety and traffic design. The problem is best dealt with in two parts: (1) the time between the decision to apply the brakes and their actual application (the "reaction time"), during which we assume $a = 0$; and (2) the actual braking period when the vehicle slows down ($a \neq 0$). The stopping distance depends on the reaction time of the driver, the initial speed of the car (the final speed is zero), and the acceleration of the car. For a dry road and good tires, good brakes can decelerate a car at a rate of about 5 m/s² to 8 m/s². Calculate the total stopping distance for an initial velocity of 100 km/h (28 m/s ≈ 62 mph) and assume the acceleration of the car is

FIGURE 2–13
Example 2–8: stopping
distance for a braking car

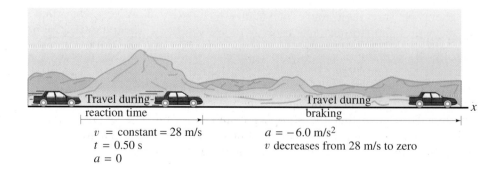

$-6.0\,\text{m/s}^2$ (the minus sign appears because the velocity is taken to be in the positive x direction and its magnitude is decreasing). Reaction time for normal drivers varies from perhaps 0.3 s to about 1.0 s; take it to be 0.50 s.

SOLUTION   The car is moving to the right in the positive x direction. We take $x_0 = 0$ for the first part of the problem, in which the car travels at a constant speed of 28 m/s during the time the driver is reacting (0.50 s). See Fig. 2–13. Thus: *Part 1: Reaction time*

Part 1:

Known	Wanted
$t = 0.50$ s	x
$v_0 = 28$ m/s	
$v = 28$ m/s	
$a = 0$	
$x_0 = 0$	

To find x we can use Eq. 2–10b (note that Eq. 2–10c isn't useful because x is multiplied by a, which is zero):

$$x = v_0 t + 0 = (28\text{ m/s})(0.50\text{ s}) = 14\text{ m}.$$

The car travels 14 m during the driver's reaction time, until the moment the brakes are applied. Now for the second part, during which the brakes are applied and the car is brought to rest. We now take $x_0 = 14$ m (result of the first part): *Part 2: Braking*

Part 2:

Known	Wanted
$x_0 = 14$ m	x
$v_0 = 28$ m/s	
$v = 0$	
$a = -6.0\text{ m/s}^2$	

Equation 2–10a doesn't contain x; Eq. 2–10b contains x but also the unknown t. Equation 2–10c is what we want; we solve for x (after setting $x_0 = 14$m):

$$v^2 - v_0^2 = 2a(x - x_0)$$

$$x = x_0 + \frac{v^2 - v_0^2}{2a}$$

$$= 14\text{ m} + \frac{0 - (28\text{ m/s})^2}{2(-6.0\text{ m/s}^2)} = 14\text{ m} + \frac{-784\text{ m}^2/\text{s}^2}{-12\text{ m/s}^2}$$

$$= 14\text{ m} + 65\text{ m} = 79\text{ m}.$$

The car traveled 14 m while the driver was reacting and another 65 m during the braking period before coming to a stop. The total distance traveled was then 79 m. Under wet or icy conditions, the value of a may be only one third the value for a dry road since the brakes cannot be applied as hard without skidding, and hence stopping distances are much greater. Note also that the stopping distance during braking increases with the *square* of the speed, not just linearly with speed. If you are traveling twice as fast, it takes four times the distance to stop.

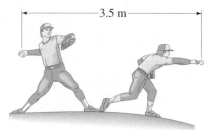

FIGURE 2–14 A baseball pitcher accelerates the ball through a displacement of about 3.5 m.

EXAMPLE 2–9 ESTIMATE **The fastball.** A baseball pitcher throws a fastball with a speed of 44 m/s. Estimate the average acceleration of the ball during the throwing motion. It is observed that in throwing the baseball, the pitcher accelerates the ball through a displacement of about 3.5 m from behind the body to the point where it is released (Fig. 2–14).

SOLUTION We want to find the acceleration a given that $x = 3.5$ m, $v_0 = 0$, and $v = 44$ m/s. We use Eq. 2–10c and solve for a:

$$a = \frac{v^2 - v_0^2}{2x}$$

$$= \frac{(44 \text{ m/s})^2 - (0 \text{ m/s})^2}{2(3.5 \text{ m})} = 280 \text{ m/s}^2.$$

This is a very large acceleration!

➡ **PHYSICS APPLIED**

Car safety—air bags

EXAMPLE 2–10 ESTIMATE **Air bags.** Suppose you want to design an air-bag system that can protect the driver in a head-on collision at a speed of 100 km/h (60 mph). Estimate how fast the air bag must inflate to effectively protect the driver. Assume the car crumples upon impact over a distance of about 1 m. How does the use of a seat belt help the driver?

SOLUTION The car decelerates from 100 km/h to zero in a very short time and a very short distance (1 m). Noting that 100 km/h $= 100 \times 10^3$ m/3600 s $= 28$ m/s, we can get the acceleration from Eq. 2–10c:

$$a = -\frac{v_0^2}{2x} = -\frac{(28 \text{ m/s})^2}{2.0 \text{ m}} = -390 \text{ m/s}^2.$$

This enormous acceleration takes place in a time given by (Eq. 2–10a):

$$t = \frac{v - v_0}{a} = \frac{0 - 28 \text{ m/s}}{-390 \text{ m/s}^2} = 0.07 \text{ s}.$$

To be effective, the air bag would need to inflate faster than this.

What does the air bag do? First, it spreads the force over a larger area of the chest. This is better than being punctured by the steering column. Also, the pressure in the bag is controlled to minimize the head's maximum deceleration. The seat belt keeps the person in the correct position against the expanding air bag.

FIGURE 2–15
Galileo Galilei (1564–1642).

The analysis of motion we have been discussing in this chapter is basically algebraic. It is sometimes helpful to use a graphical interpretation as well, and this is discussed in the optional Section 2–8.

2–7 Falling Objects

One of the most common examples of uniformly accelerated motion is that of an object allowed to fall freely near the Earth's surface. That a falling object is accelerating may not be obvious at first. And beware of thinking, as was widely believed until the time of Galileo (Fig. 2–15), that heavier objects fall faster than lighter objects and that the speed of fall is proportional to how heavy the object is.

Galileo's analysis made use of his new and creative technique of imagining what would happen in idealized (simplified) cases. For free fall, he postulated that all objects would fall with the *same constant acceleration* in the absence of air or other resistance. He showed that this postulate predicts that for an object falling from rest, the distance traveled will be proportional to the square of the time (Fig. 2–16); that is, $d \propto t^2$. We can see this from Eq. 2–10b, but Galileo was the first to derive this mathematical relation. In fact, among Galileo's great contributions to science was to establish such mathematical relations, and to insist on their importance. Another great contribution of Galileo was to propose theories with specific experimental consequences that could be quantitatively checked (such as $d \propto t^2$).

To support his claim that the speed of falling objects increases as they fall, Galileo made use of a clever argument: a heavy stone dropped from a height of 2 m will drive a stake into the ground much further than will the same stone dropped from a height of only 0.2 m. Clearly, the stone must be moving faster in the former case.

As we saw, Galileo also claimed that *all* objects, light or heavy, fall with the *same* acceleration, at least in the absence of air. If you hold a piece of paper horizontally in one hand and a heavier object—say, a baseball—in the other, and release them at the same time as in Fig. 2–17a, the heavier object will reach the ground first. But if you repeat the experiment, this time crumpling the paper into a small wad (see Fig. 2–17b), you will find that the two objects reach the floor at nearly the same time.

Galileo was sure that air acts as a resistance to very light objects that have a large surface area. But in many ordinary circumstances this air resistance is negligible. In a chamber from which the air has been removed, even light objects like a feather or a horizontally held piece of paper will fall with the same acceleration as any other object (see Fig. 2–18). Such a demonstration in vacuum was of course not possible in Galileo's time, which makes Galileo's achievement all the greater. Galileo is often called the "father of modern science," not only for the content of his science (astronomical discoveries, inertia, free fall), but also for his style or approach to science (idealization and simplification, mathematization of theory, theories that have testable consequences, experiments to test theoretical predictions).

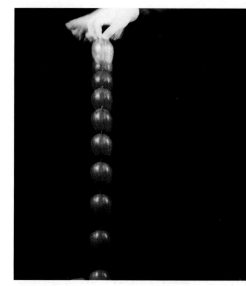

FIGURE 2–16 Multiflash photograph of a falling apple, photographed at equal time intervals. Note that the apple falls farther during each successive time interval, which means it is accelerating.

FIGURE 2–17 (a) A ball and a light piece of paper are dropped at the same time. (b) Repeated, with the paper wadded up.

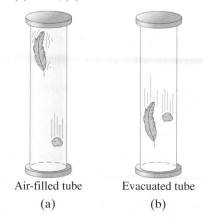

FIGURE 2–18 A rock and a feather are dropped simultaneously (a) in air, (b) in a vacuum.

Air-filled tube   Evacuated tube

(a)   (b)

Galileo's specific contribution to our understanding of the motion of falling objects can be summarized as follows:

Galileo's hypothesis: free fall is at constant acceleration g

at a given location on the Earth and in the absence of air resistance, all objects fall with the same constant acceleration.

We call this acceleration the **acceleration due to gravity** on the Earth, and we give it the symbol g. Its magnitude is approximately

$$g = 9.80 \text{ m/s}^2.$$

In British units g is about 32 ft/s^2. Actually, g varies slightly according to latitude and elevation (see Table 2–1), but these variations are so small that we will ignore them for most purposes. The effects of air resistance are often small, and we will neglect them for the most part. However, air resistance will be noticeable even on a reasonably heavy object if the velocity becomes large.[†]

When dealing with freely falling objects we can make use of Eqs. 2–10, where for a we use the value of g given above. Also, since the motion is vertical we will substitute y in place of x, and y_0 in place of x_0. We take $y_0 = 0$ unless otherwise specified. *It is arbitrary whether we choose y to be positive in the upward direction or in the downward direction; but we must be consistent about it throughout a problem's solution.*

TABLE 2–1
Acceleration Due to Gravity at Various Locations on Earth

Location	Elevation (m)	g (m/s²)
New York	0	9.803
San Francisco	100	9.800
Denver	1650	9.796
Pikes Peak	4300	9.789
Equator	0	9.780
North Pole (calculated)	0	9.832

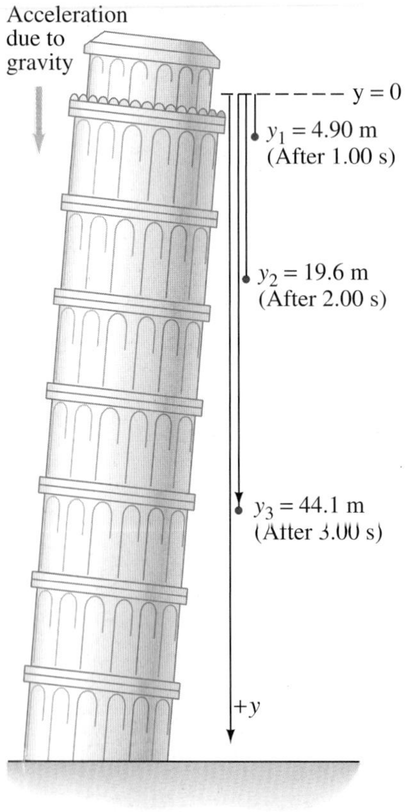

FIGURE 2–19 Example 2–11. When an object is dropped from a tower, it falls with progressively greater speed and covers greater distance with each successive second. (See also Fig. 2–16.)

Acceleration due to gravity

$y = 0$

$y_1 = 4.90$ m (After 1.00 s)

$y_2 = 19.6$ m (After 2.00 s)

$y_3 = 44.1$ m (After 3.00 s)

$+y$

EXAMPLE 2–11 **Falling from a tower.** Suppose that a ball is dropped from a tower 70.0 m high. How far will it have fallen after 1.00 s, 2.00 s, and 3.00 s? Assume y is positive downward. Neglect air resistance.

SOLUTION We are given the acceleration, $a = g = +9.80 \text{ m/s}^2$, which is positive because we have chosen downward as positive. Since we want to find the distance fallen given the time, t, Eq. 2–10b is the appropriate one, with $v_0 = 0$ and $y_0 = 0$. Then, after 1.00 s, the position of the ball is

$$y_1 = \tfrac{1}{2}at^2 = \tfrac{1}{2}(9.80 \text{ m/s}^2)(1.00 \text{ s})^2 = 4.90 \text{ m},$$

so the ball has fallen a distance of 4.90 m after 1.00 s. Similarly, after 2.00 s,

$$y_2 = \tfrac{1}{2}at^2 = \tfrac{1}{2}(9.80 \text{ m/s}^2)(2.00 \text{ s})^2 = 19.6 \text{ m},$$

and after 3.00 s,

$$y_3 = \tfrac{1}{2}at^2 = \tfrac{1}{2}(9.80 \text{ m/s}^2)(3.00 \text{ s})^2 = 44.1 \text{ m}.$$

See Fig. 2–19.

EXAMPLE 2–12 **Thrown down from a tower.** Suppose the ball in Example 2–11 is *thrown* downward with an initial velocity of 3.00 m/s, instead of being dropped. (*a*) What then would be its position after 1.00 s and 2.00 s? (*b*) What would its speed be after 1.00 s and 2.00 s? Compare to the speeds of a dropped ball.

[†]The speed of an object falling in air (or other fluid) does not increase indefinitely. If the object falls far enough, it will reach a maximum velocity called the **terminal velocity**. Acceleration due to gravity is a vector (as is any acceleration), and its direction is downward, toward the center of the Earth.

SOLUTION (*a*) We can approach this in the same way as Example 2–11, using Eq. 2–10b, but this time v_0 is not zero but is $v_0 = 3.0 \text{ m/s}$. Thus, at $t = 1.00 \text{ s}$, the position of the ball is

$$y = v_0 t + \tfrac{1}{2} a t^2 = (3.00 \text{ m/s})(1.00 \text{ s}) + \tfrac{1}{2}(9.80 \text{ m/s}^2)(1.00 \text{ s})^2 = 7.90 \text{ m},$$

and at $t = 2.00 \text{ s}$

$$y = v_0 t + \tfrac{1}{2} a t^2 = (3.00 \text{ m/s})(2.00 \text{ s}) + \tfrac{1}{2}(9.80 \text{ m/s}^2)(2.00 \text{ s})^2 = 25.6 \text{ m}.$$

As expected, the ball falls farther each second than if it were dropped with $v_0 = 0$.

(*b*) The velocity is readily obtained from Eq. 2–10a:

$$v = v_0 + at$$

$$= 3.00 \text{ m/s} + (9.80 \text{ m/s}^2)(1.00 \text{ s}) = 12.8 \text{ m/s} \quad [\text{at } t = 1.00 \text{ s}]$$

$$= 3.00 \text{ m/s} + (9.80 \text{ m/s}^2)(2.00 \text{ s}) = 22.6 \text{ m/s}. \quad [\text{at } t = 2.00 \text{ s}]$$

When the ball is dropped ($v_0 = 0$), the first term in the above equations is zero, so

$$v = 0 + at$$

$$= (9.80 \text{ m/s}^2)(1.00 \text{ s}) = 9.80 \text{ m/s} \quad [\text{at } t = 1.00 \text{ s}]$$

$$= (9.80 \text{ m/s}^2)(2.00 \text{ s}) = 19.6 \text{ m/s}. \quad [\text{at } t = 2.00 \text{ s}]$$

We see that the speed of a dropped ball increases linearly in time. (In Example 2–11 we saw that the distance fallen increases as the *square* of the time.) The downwardly thrown ball also increases linearly in speed ($\Delta v = 9.80 \text{ m/s}$ each second), but its speed at any moment is always 3.0 m/s (its initial speed) higher than a falling ball.

EXAMPLE 2–13 **Ball thrown upward.** A person throws a ball *upward* into the air with an initial velocity of 15.0 m/s. Calculate (*a*) how high it goes, and (*b*) how long the ball is in the air before it comes back to his hand. We are not concerned here with the throwing action, but only with the motion of the ball *after* it leaves the thrower's hand (Fig. 2–20).

SOLUTION Let us choose y to be positive in the upward direction and negative in the downward direction. (Note: This is a different convention from that used in Examples 2–11 and 2–12.) Then the acceleration due to gravity will have a negative sign, $a = -9.80 \text{ m/s}^2$. Note that as the ball rises, its speed decreases until it reaches the highest point (B in Fig. 2–20), where its speed is zero for an instant; then it descends with increasing speed.

(*a*) To determine the maximum height, we calculate the position of the ball when its velocity equals zero ($v = 0$ at the highest point). At $t = 0$ (point A in Fig. 2–20) we have $y_0 = 0$, $v_0 = 15.0 \text{ m/s}$, and $a = -9.80 \text{ m/s}^2$. At time t (maximum height), $v = 0$, $a = -9.80 \text{ m/s}^2$, and we wish to find y. We use Eq. 2–10c (replacing x with y) and solve for y:

$$v^2 = v_0^2 + 2ay$$

$$y = \frac{v^2 - v_0^2}{2a} = \frac{0 - (15.0 \text{ m/s})^2}{2(-9.80 \text{ m/s}^2)} = 11.5 \text{ m}.$$

The ball reaches a height of 11.5 m above the hand.

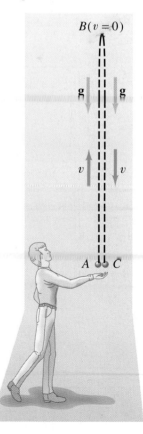

FIGURE 2–20 An object thrown into the air leaves the thrower's hand at A, reaches its maximum height at B, and returns to the original height at C. Examples 2–13, 2–14, and 2–15.

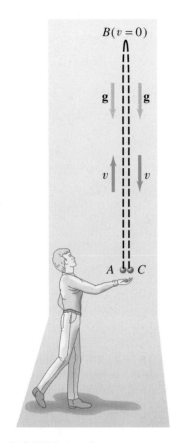

$B (v = 0)$

g g

v v

A C

FIGURE 2–21 Examples 2–13, 2–14, and 2–15.

(b) Now we need to calculate how long the ball is in the air before it returns to his hand. We could do this calculation in two parts by first determining the time required for the ball to reach its highest point, and then determining the time it takes to fall back down. However, it is simpler to consider the motion from A to B to C (Fig. 2–21) in one step and use Eq. 2–10b. We can do this because y (or x) represents position or displacement, and not the total distance traveled. Thus, at both points A and C, $y = 0$. We use Eq. 2–10b with $a = -9.80\ \text{m/s}^2$ and find

$$y = v_0 t + \tfrac{1}{2} a t^2$$

$$0 = (15.0\ \text{m/s})t + \tfrac{1}{2}(-9.80\ \text{m/s}^2)t^2.$$

This equation is readily factored (we factor out one t):

$$(15.0\ \text{m/s} - 4.90\ \text{m/s}^2\, t)\, t = 0.$$

There are two solutions:

$$t = 0,$$

and

$$t = \frac{15.0\ \text{m/s}}{4.90\ \text{m/s}^2} = 3.06\ \text{s}.$$

The first solution ($t = 0$) corresponds to the initial point (A) in Fig. 2–21, when the ball was first thrown and was also at $y = 0$. The second solution, $t = 3.06\ \text{s}$, corresponds to point C, when the ball has returned to $y = 0$. Thus the ball is in the air 3.06 s.

Careful:
Velocity and acceleration are not always in the same direction

Careful:
$a \neq 0$ even at the highest point of a trajectory

CONCEPTUAL EXAMPLE 2–14 | **Two common misconceptions.** Explain the error in these two common misconceptions: (1) that acceleration and velocity are always in the same direction, and (2) that an object thrown upward has zero acceleration at the highest point (B in Fig. 2–21).

RESPONSE Both are wrong. (1) Velocity and acceleration are *not* necessarily in the same direction. When the ball in Example 2–13 is moving upward, its velocity is positive (upward), whereas the acceleration is negative (downward). (2) At the highest point (B in Fig. 2–21), the ball has zero velocity for an instant. Is the acceleration also zero at this point? No. Gravity does not stop acting, so $a = -g = -9.80\ \text{m/s}^2$ even there. Thinking that $a = 0$ at point B would lead to the conclusion that upon reaching point B, the ball would hover there. For if the acceleration (=rate of change of velocity) were zero, the velocity would remain zero, and the ball could stay up there without falling.

EXAMPLE 2–15 **Ball thrown upward, II.** Let us consider again the ball thrown upward of Example 2–13, and make three more calculations. Calculate (a) how much time it takes for the ball to reach the maximum height (point B in Fig. 2–21), (b) the velocity of the ball when it returns to the thrower's hand (point C), and (c) at what time t the ball passes a point 8.00 m above the person's hand.

SOLUTION Again we take y as positive upward. (a) Both Eqs. 2–10a and 2–10b contain the time t with other quantities known. Let us use Eq. 2–10a with $a = -9.80 \text{ m/s}^2$, $v_0 = 15.0 \text{ m/s}$, and $v = 0$:

$$v = v_0 + at,$$

so

$$t = -\frac{v_0}{a} = -\frac{15.0 \text{ m/s}}{-9.80 \text{ m/s}^2} = 1.53 \text{ s}.$$

This is just half the time it takes the ball to go up and fall back to its original position [3.06 s, calculated in part (b) of Example 2–13]. Thus it takes the same time to reach the maximum height as to fall back to the starting point. (b) We use Eq. 2–10a with $v_0 = 15.0 \text{ m/s}$ and $t = 3.06 \text{ s}$ (the time calculated in Example 2–13 for the ball to come back to the hand):

$$v = v_0 + at = 15.0 \text{ m/s} - (9.80 \text{ m/s}^2)(3.06 \text{ s}) = -15.0 \text{ m/s}.$$

The ball has the same magnitude of velocity when it returns to the starting point as it did initially, but in the opposite direction (this is the meaning of the negative sign). Thus, as we gathered from part (a), we see that the motion is symmetrical about the maximum height.
(c) We want t, given that $y = 8.00 \text{ m}$, $y_0 = 0$, $v_0 = 15.0 \text{ m/s}$, and $a = -9.80 \text{ m/s}^2$. We use Eq. 2–10b:

Note the symmetry: the speed at any height is the same when going up as coming down (but the direction is opposite)

$$y = y_0 + v_0 t + \tfrac{1}{2}at^2$$

$$0.00 \text{ m} = 0 + (15.0 \text{ m/s})t + \tfrac{1}{2}(-9.80 \text{ m/s}^2)t^2$$

To solve any quadratic equation of the form $at^2 + bt + c = 0$, where a, b, and c are constants, we can use the **quadratic formula** (see Appendix A–4):

$$t = \frac{-b \pm \sqrt{b^2 - 4ac}}{2a}.$$

➡ **PROBLEM SOLVING**

Using the quadratic formula

We rewrite our equation in standard form:

$$(4.90 \text{ m/s}^2)t^2 - (15.0 \text{ m/s})t + (8.00 \text{ m}) = 0.$$

So the coefficient a is 4.90 m/s^2, b is -15.0 m/s, and c is 8.00 m. Putting these into the quadratic formula, we obtain

$$t = \frac{15.0 \text{ m/s} \pm \sqrt{(15.0 \text{ m/s})^2 - 4(4.90 \text{ m/s}^2)(8.00 \text{ m})}}{2(4.90 \text{ m/s}^2)},$$

so $t = 0.69 \text{ s}$ and $t = 2.37 \text{ s}$. Why are there two solutions? Are they both valid? Yes, because the ball passes $y = 8.00 \text{ m}$ when it goes up ($t = 0.69 \text{ s}$) and again when it comes down ($t = 2.37 \text{ s}$).

Acceleration expressed in g's

The acceleration of an object, particularly rockets and fast airplanes, is often given as a multiple of $g = 9.80 \text{ m/s}^2$. For example, a plane pulling out of a dive and undergoing $3.00\,g$'s would have an acceleration of $(3.00)(9.80 \text{ m/s}^2) = 29.4 \text{ m/s}^2$.

* 2–8 Graphical Analysis of Linear Motion[†]

Figure 2–8 showed the graph of the velocity of a car versus time for two cases of linear motion: (*a*) constant velocity, and (*b*) a particular case in which the magnitude of the velocity varied. It is also useful to graph (or "plot") the position x as a function of time. The time t is considered the independent variable and is measured along the horizontal axis. The position, x, the dependent variable, is measured along the vertical axis.

We make a graph of x vs. t, and we make the choice that at $t = 0$, the position is $x_0 = 0$. First we consider a car moving at a constant velocity of 40 km/h, which is equivalent to 11 m/s. From Eq. 2–10b, $x = vt$, and we see that x increases by 11 m every second. Thus, the position increases linearly in time, so the graph of x vs. t is a straight line, as shown in Fig. 2–22. Each point on this straight line tells us the car's position at a particular time. For example, at $t = 3.0$ s, the position is 33 m, and at $t = 4.0$ s, $x = 44$ m, as indicated by the dashed lines. The small triangle on the graph indicates the **slope** of the straight line, which is defined as the change in the dependent variable (Δx) divided by the corresponding change in the independent variable (Δt):

$$\text{slope} = \frac{\Delta x}{\Delta t}.$$

We see, using the definition of velocity (Eq. 2–2), that the slope of the x vs. t graph is equal to the velocity. And, as can be seen from the small tri-

[†]Some sections of this book, such as this one, may be considered *optional* at the discretion of the instructor. See the Preface for more details.

FIGURE 2–22 Graph of position vs. time for an object moving at a uniform velocity of 11 m/s.

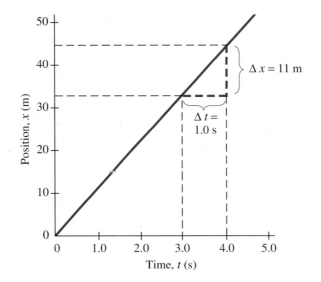

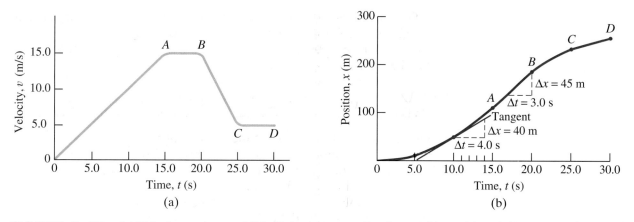

FIGURE 2–23 (a) Velocity vs. time and (b) displacement vs. time for an object with variable velocity. (See text.)

angle on the graph, $\Delta x/\Delta t = (11\,\text{m})/(1.0\,\text{s}) = 11\,\text{m/s}$, which is the given velocity.

The slope of the x vs. t graph is everywhere the same if the velocity is constant, as in Fig. 2–22. But if the velocity changes, as in Fig. 2–23, the slope of the x vs. t graph also varies. Consider, for example, a car that accelerates uniformly from rest to $15\,\text{m/s}$ in $15\,\text{s}$, after which it remains at a constant velocity of $15\,\text{m/s}$ for the next $5.0\,\text{s}$, then slows down uniformly to $5.0\,\text{m/s}$ during the following $5.0\,\text{s}$, and then remains at this constant velocity. The velocity as a function of time is shown in the graph of Fig. 2–23a. Now, to construct the x vs. t graph, we can use Eq. 2–10b with constant acceleration for the intervals $t = 0$ to $t = 15\,\text{s}$ and $t = 20\,\text{s}$ to $t = 25\,\text{s}$, and with constant velocity for the periods $t = 15\,\text{s}$ to $t = 20\,\text{s}$ and after $t = 25\,\text{s}$. The result is the x vs. t graph of Fig. 2–23b.

From the origin to point A on the plot, the x vs. t graph is not a straight line, but a curve. The **slope** of the curve at any point is defined as the *slope of the tangent to the curve at that point.* (The *tangent* is a straight line drawn so it touches the curve only at that one point, but does not pass across or through the curve.) For example, the tangent to the curve at the time $t = 10.0\,\text{s}$ is drawn on the graph (it is labeled "tangent"). A triangle is drawn with Δt chosen to be $4.0\,\text{s}$; Δx can be measured off the graph for this chosen Δt and is found to be $40\,\text{m}$. Thus, the slope of the curve at $t = 10.0\,\text{s}$, which equals the instantaneous velocity at that instant, is $v = \Delta x/\Delta t = 40\,\text{m}/4.0\,\text{s} = 10\,\text{m/s}$. In the region between A and B (Fig. 2–23) the x vs. t graph is a straight line and the slope can be measured using the triangle shown between $t = 17\,\text{s}$ and $t = 20\,\text{s}$, where the increase in x is $45\,\text{m}$: $\Delta x/\Delta t = 45\,\text{m}/3.0\,\text{s} = 15\,\text{m/s}$.

Suppose we were given the x vs. t graph of Fig. 2–23b. We could measure the slopes at a number of points and plot these slopes as a function of time. Since the slope equals the velocity, we could thus reconstruct the v vs. t graph! In other words, given the graph of x vs. t, we can determine the velocity as a function of time using graphical methods, instead of using equations. This technique is particularly useful when the acceleration is not constant, for then Eqs. 2–10 cannot be used.

Slope of a curve

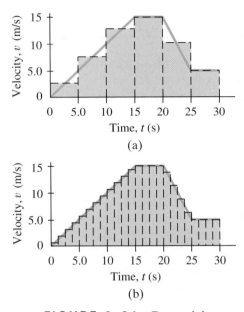

FIGURE 2–24 Determining the displacement from the graph of v vs. t is done by calculating areas.

Displacement = area under v vs. t graph

The reverse process is also possible. If we are given the v vs. t graph, we can determine the position, x, as a function of time. To do so, we use the following procedure, which we apply to the v vs. t graph of Fig. 2–24a (which is the same as Fig. 2–23a). We first divide the time axis into many subintervals (in Fig. 2–24a, only six for simplicity), which are indicated in the figure by the dashed vertical lines. In each interval, a *horizontal* dashed line is drawn to indicate the average velocity during that time interval. For example, in the first interval, the velocity increases at a constant rate from zero to 5.0 m/s, so $\bar{v} = 2.5$ m/s; and in the fourth interval the velocity is a constant 15 m/s, so $\bar{v} = 15$ m/s (no horizontal dashed line is shown since it coincides with the curve itself). The displacement (change in position) during any subinterval is $\Delta x = \bar{v}\Delta t$. Thus the displacement during each subinterval equals the product of $\bar{v}$ and Δt, and this is just the *area of the rectangle* (base × height = $\Delta t \times v$), shown shaded in rose, for that interval. The total displacement after 25 s, say, will be the sum of the first five rectangles.

If the velocity varies a great deal, it may be difficult to estimate $\bar{v}$ from the graph. To reduce this difficulty, more—but narrower—subintervals are used. That is, we make each Δt smaller, as in Fig. 2–24b. The more intervals give a better approximation. Ideally, we could let Δt approach zero; this leads to the techniques of integral calculus, which we don't discuss here. The result, in any case, is that *the total displacement between any two times is equal to the area under the v vs. t graph between these two times*.

EXAMPLE 2–16 **Displacement from graph.** A space probe accelerates uniformly from 50 m/s at $t = 0$ to 150 m/s at $t = 10$ s. How far did it move between $t = 2.0$ s and $t = 6.0$ s?

SOLUTION A graph of v vs. t can be drawn as shown in Fig. 2–25. We simply need to calculate the area of the shaded region shown in rose, which is a trapezoid. The area will be the average of the heights (in units of velocity) times the width (which is 4.0 s). At $t = 2.0$ s, $v = 70$ m/s; and at $t = 6.0$ s, $v = 110$ m/s. Thus the area, which equals Δx, is

$$\Delta x = \left(\frac{70 \text{ m/s} + 110 \text{ m/s}}{2}\right)(4.0 \text{ s}) = 360 \text{ m}.$$

For this case of constant acceleration, we could use Eqs. 2–10 and we would get the same result: $a = \Delta v/\Delta t = (150 \text{ m/s} - 50 \text{ m/s})/10 \text{ s} = 10$ m/s; at $t = 2.0$ s, $v = v_0 + at = 50$ m/s $+ (10 \text{ m/s}^2)(2.0 \text{ s}) = 70$ m/s, and at $t = 6.0$ s, $v = 50$ m/s $+ (10 \text{ m/s}^2)(6.0 \text{ s}) = 110$ m/s; then, using Eq. 2–10c,

$$\Delta x = \frac{(v^2 - v_0^2)}{2a}$$

$$= \frac{(110 \text{ m/s})^2 - (70 \text{ m/s})^2}{2(10 \text{ m/s}^2)} = 360 \text{ m}.$$

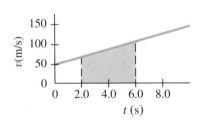

FIGURE 2–25 Example 2–16: the rose-shaded area represents the displacement during the time interval $t = 2.0$ s to $t = 6.0$ s.

In cases where the acceleration is not constant, the area can be obtained by counting squares on graph paper.

SUMMARY

[The Summary that appears at the end of each chapter in this book gives a brief overview of the main ideas of the chapter. The Summary *cannot* serve to give an understanding of the material, which can be accomplished only by a detailed reading of the chapter.]

Kinematics deals with the description of how objects move. The description of the motion of any object must always be given relative to some particular **reference frame**.

The **displacement** of an object is the change in position of the object.

Average speed is the distance traveled divided by the elapsed time. An object's **average velocity** over a particular time interval Δt is the displacement Δx divided by Δt:

$$\bar{v} = \frac{\Delta x}{\Delta t}.$$

The **instantaneous velocity**, whose magnitude is the same as the *instantaneous speed*, is the average velocity taken over an infinitesimally short time interval.

Acceleration is the change of velocity per unit time. An object's **average acceleration** over a time interval Δt is

$$\bar{a} = \frac{\Delta v}{\Delta t},$$

where Δv is the change of velocity during the time interval Δt. **Instantaneous acceleration** is the average acceleration taken over an infinitesimally short time interval.

If an object moves in a straight line with constant acceleration, the velocity v and position x are related to the acceleration a, the elapsed time t, and the initial position x_0 and initial velocity v_0, by Eqs. 2–10:

$$v = v_0 + at, \qquad\qquad x = x_0 + v_0 t + \tfrac{1}{2}at^2,$$

$$v^2 = v_0^2 + 2a(x - x_0), \qquad\qquad \bar{v} = \frac{v + v_0}{2}.$$

Objects that move vertically near the surface of the Earth, either falling or having been projected vertically up or down, move with the constant downward **acceleration due to gravity** with magnitude of about $g = 9.80\ \text{m/s}^2$, if air resistance can be ignored.

QUESTIONS

1. Does a car speedometer measure speed, velocity, or both?

2. Can an object have a varying velocity if its speed is constant? If yes, give examples.

3. Can an object have a varying speed if its velocity is constant? If yes, give examples.

4. When an object moves with constant velocity, does its average velocity during any time interval differ from its instantaneous velocity at any instant?

5. In drag racing, is it possible for the car with the greatest speed crossing the finish line to lose the race? Explain.

6. If one object has a greater speed than a second object, does the first necessarily have a greater acceleration? Explain, using examples.

7. Compare the acceleration of a motorcycle that accelerates from 80 km/h to 90 km/h with the acceleration of a bicycle that accelerates from rest to 10 km/h in the same time.

8. How is speed represented on a speedometer? How is acceleration represented?

9. Can an object have a northward velocity and a southward acceleration? Explain.

10. Can the velocity of an object be negative when its acceleration is positive? What about vice versa?

11. Give an example where both the velocity and acceleration are negative.

12. Is it possible for an object to have a negative acceleration while increasing in speed? If so, provide an example.

13. Two cars emerge side by side from a tunnel. Car A is traveling with a speed of 60 km/h and has an acceleration of 40 km/h/min. Car B has a speed of 40 km/h and has an acceleration of 60 km/h/min. Which car is passing the other as they come out of the tunnel? Explain your reasoning.

14. Can an object be increasing in speed as its acceleration decreases? If so, give an example. If not, explain.

15. As a freely falling object speeds up, what is happening to its acceleration due to gravity? Does it increase, decrease, or stay the same?

16. How would you estimate the maximum height you could throw a ball vertically upward? How would you estimate the maximum speed you could give it?

17. An object that is thrown vertically upward will return to its original position with the same speed as it had initially if air resistance is negligible. If air resistance is appreciable, will this result be altered, and if so, how? [*Hint*: The acceleration due to air resistance is always in a direction opposite to the motion.]

* 18. Describe in words the motion plotted in Fig. 2–26 in terms of v, a, etc. [*Hint*: First try to duplicate the motion plotted by walking or moving your hand.]

* 19. Describe in words the motion of the object graphed in Fig. 2–27.

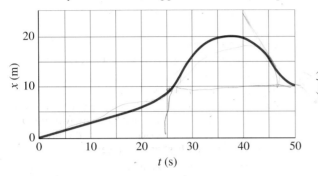

FIGURE 2–26 Question 18, Problems 51, 52, and 57.

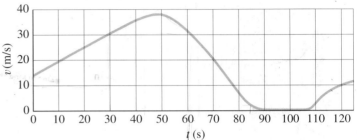

FIGURE 2–27 Question 19, Problems 53, 56, and 58.

■ PROBLEMS

[The problems at the end of each chapter are ranked I, II, or III according to estimated difficulty, with I problems being easiest. The problems are arranged by Section, meaning that the reader should have read up to and including that Section, but not only that Section—problems often depend on earlier material. Finally, there is a set of unranked "General Problems" not arranged by Section number.]

SECTIONS 2–1 TO 2–3

1. (I) What must be your average speed in order to travel 230 km in 3.25 h?

2. (I) A bird can fly 25 km/h. How long does it take to fly 15 km?

3. (I) If you are driving 110 km/h along a straight road and you look to the side for 2.0 s, how far do you travel during this inattentive period?

4. (I) 65 mph is how many (*a*) km/h, (*b*) m/s, and (*c*) ft/s?

5. (II) You are driving home from school steadily at 65 mph for 130 miles. It then begins to rain and you slow to 55 mph. You arrive home after driving 3 hours and 20 minutes. (*a*) How far is your hometown from school? (*b*) What was your average speed?

6. (II) According to a rule-of-thumb, every five seconds between a lightning flash and the following thunder gives the distance of the storm in miles. Assuming that the flash of light arrives in essentially no time at all, estimate the speed of sound in m/s from this rule.

7. (II) A person jogs eight complete laps around a quarter-mile track in a total time of 12.5 min. Calculate (*a*) the average speed and (*b*) the average velocity, in m/s.

8. (II) A horse canters away from its trainer in a straight line, moving 130 m away in 14.0 s. It then turns abruptly and gallops halfway back in 4.8 s. Calculate (*a*) its average speed and (*b*) its average velocity for the entire trip, using "away from the trainer" as the positive direction.

9. (II) Two locomotives approach each other on parallel tracks. Each has a speed of 95 km/h with respect to the ground. If they are initially 8.5 km apart, how long will it be before they reach each other? (See Fig. 2–28.)

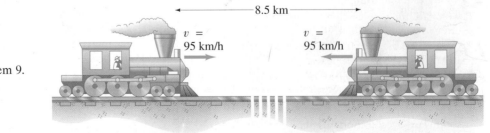

FIGURE 2–28 Problem 9.

10. (II) An airplane travels 2100 km at a speed of 800 km/h, and then encounters a tailwind that boosts its speed to 1000 km/h for the next 1800 km. What was the total time for the trip? What was the average speed of the plane for this trip? [Hint: Think carefully before using Eq. 2–10d.]

11. (II) Calculate the average speed and average velocity of a complete round-trip in which the outgoing 200 km is covered at 90 km/h, followed by a one-hour lunch break, and the return 200 km is covered at 50 km/h.

12. (III) A bowling ball traveling with constant speed hits the pins at the end of a bowling lane 16.5 m long. The bowler hears the sound of the ball hitting the pins 2.50 s after the ball is released from his hands. What is the speed of the ball? The speed of sound is 340 m/s.

SECTION 2–4

13. (I) A sports car accelerates from rest to 95 km/h in 6.2 s. What is its average acceleration in m/s^2?

14. (I) At highway speeds, a particular automobile is capable of an acceleration of about $1.6 \, m/s^2$. At this rate, how long does it take to accelerate from 80 km/h to 110 km/h?

15. (I) A sprinter accelerates from rest to 10.0 m/s in 1.35 s. What is her acceleration (a) in m/s^2, and (b) in km/h^2?

16. (II) A sports car is advertised to be able to stop in a distance of 50 m from a speed of 90 km/h. What is its acceleration in m/s^2? How many g's is this ($g = 9.80 \, m/s^2$)?

17. (III) The position of a racing car, which starts from rest at $t = 0$ and moves in a straight line, has been measured as a function of time, as given in the following table. Estimate (a) its velocity and (b) its acceleration as a function of time. Display each in a table and on a graph.

$t(s)$	0	0.25	0.50	0.75	1.00	1.50	2.00	2.50
$x(m)$	0	0.11	0.46	1.06	1.94	4.62	8.55	13.79

$t(s)$	3.00	3.50	4.00	4.50	5.00	5.50	6.00
$x(m)$	20.36	28.31	37.65	48.37	60.30	73.26	87.16

SECTIONS 2–5 AND 2–6

18. (I) The principal kinematic equations, Eqs. 2–10a through 2–10d, become particularly simple if the initial speed is zero. Write down the equations for this special case. (Also put $x_0 = 0$.)

19. (I) A car accelerates from 12 m/s to 25 m/s in 6.0 s. What was its acceleration? How far did it travel in this time? Assume constant acceleration.

20. (I) A car slows down from 20 m/s to rest in a distance of 85 m. What was its acceleration, assumed constant?

21. (I) A light plane must reach a speed of 30 m/s for takeoff. How long a runway is needed if the (constant) acceleration is $3.0 \, m/s^2$?

22. (II) A world-class sprinter can burst out of the blocks to essentially top speed (of about 11.5 m/s) in the first 15.0 m of the race. What is the average acceleration of this sprinter and how long does it take her to reach that speed?

23. (II) A car slows down from a speed of 25.0 m/s to rest in 5.00 s. How far did it travel in that time?

24. (II) In coming to a stop, a car leaves skid marks 80 m long on the highway. Assuming a deceleration of $7.00 \, m/s^2$, estimate the speed of the car just before braking.

25. (II) A car traveling 45 km/h slows down at a constant $0.50 \, m/s^2$ just by "letting up on the gas." Calculate (a) the distance the car coasts before it stops, (b) the time it takes to stop, and (c) the distance it travels during the first and fifth seconds.

26. (II) A car traveling at 90 km/h strikes a tree. The front end of the car compresses and the driver comes to rest after traveling 0.80 m. What was the average acceleration of the driver during the collision? Express the answer in terms of "g's," where $1.00 \, g = 9.80 \, m/s^2$.

27. (II) Determine the stopping distances for an automobile with an initial speed of 90 km/h and human reaction time of 1.0 s: (a) for an acceleration $a = -4.0 \, m/s^2$; (b) for $a = -8.0 \, m/s^2$.

28. (III) Show that the equation for the stopping distance of a car is $d_S = v_0 t_R - v_0^2/(2a)$, where v_0 is the initial speed of the car, t_R is the driver's reaction time, and a is the constant acceleration (and is negative).

29. (III) A speeding motorist traveling 120 km/h passes a stationary police officer. The officer immediately begins pursuit at a constant acceleration of 10.0 km/h/s (note the mixed units). How much time will it take for the police officer to reach the speeder, assuming that the speeder maintains a constant speed? How fast will the police officer be traveling at this time?

30. (III) A person driving her car at 50 km/h approaches an intersection just as the traffic light turns yellow. She knows that the yellow light lasts only 2.0 s before turning to red, and she is 30 m away from the near side of the intersection (Fig. 2–29). Should she try to stop, or should she make a run for it? The intersection is 15 m wide. Her car's maximum deceleration is $-6.0 \, m/s^2$, whereas it can accelerate from 50 km/h to 70 km/h in 6.0 s. Ignore the length of her car and her reaction time.

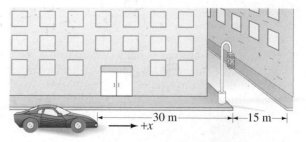

FIGURE 2–29 Problem 30.

31. (III) A runner hopes to complete the 10,000-m run in less than 30.0 min. After exactly 27.0 min, there are still 1100 m to go. The runner must then accelerate at 0.20 m/s^2 for how many seconds in order to achieve the desired time?

SECTION 2–7 [neglect air resistance]

32. (I) Calculate the acceleration of the baseball in Example 2–9 in "g's."

33. (I) If a car rolls gently ($v_0 = 0$) off a vertical cliff, how long does it take it to reach 90 km/h?

34. (I) A stone is dropped from the top of a cliff. It is seen to hit the ground below after 3.50 s. How high is the cliff?

35. (I) Calculate (a) how long it took King Kong to fall straight down from the top of the Empire State Building (380 m high), and (b) his velocity just before "landing"?

36. (II) A foul ball is hit straight up into the air with a speed of about 25 m/s. (a) How high does it go? (b) How long is it in the air?

37. (II) A kangaroo jumps to a vertical height of 2.7 m. How long was it in the air before returning to Earth?

38. (II) A ballplayer catches a ball 3.3 s after throwing it vertically upward. With what speed did he throw it, and what height did it reach?

39. (II) Draw graphs of (a) the speed and (b) the distance fallen, as a function of time, for an object falling under the influence of gravity from $t = 0$ to $t = 5.00$ s. Ignore air resistance and assume $v_0 = 0$.

40. (II) The best rebounders in basketball have a vertical leap (that is, the vertical movement of a fixed point on their body) of about 120 cm. (a) What is their initial "launch" speed off the ground? (b) How long are they in the air?

41. (II) A helicopter is ascending vertically with a speed of 5.50 m/s. At a height of 105 m above the Earth, a package is dropped from a window. How much time does it take for the package to reach the ground?

42. (II) For an object falling freely from rest, show that the distance traveled during each successive second increases in the ratio of successive odd integers (1, 3, 5, etc.). (This was first shown by Galileo.) See Figs. 2–16 and 2–19.

43. (II) If air resistance is neglected, show (algebraically) that a ball thrown vertically upward with a speed v_0 will have the same speed, v_0, when it comes back down to the starting point.

44. (II) A stone is thrown vertically upward with a speed of 20.0 m/s. (a) How fast is it moving when it reaches a height of 12.0 m? (b) How long is required to reach this height? (c) Why are there two answers to (b)?

45. (II) Estimate the time between each photoflash of the apple in Fig. 2–16 (or number of photoflashes per second). Assume the apple is about 10 cm in diameter.

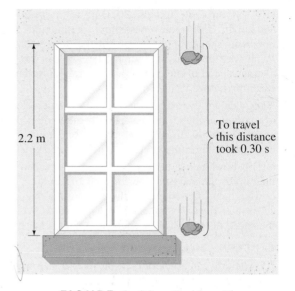

FIGURE 2–30   Problem 46.

46. (III) A falling stone takes 0.30 s to travel past a window 2.2 m tall (Fig. 2–30). From what height above the top of the window did the stone fall?

47. (III) A rock is dropped from a sea cliff and the sound of it striking the ocean is heard 3.4 s later. If the speed of sound is 340 m/s, how high is the cliff?

48. (III) Suppose you adjust your garden hose nozzle for a hard stream of water. You point the nozzle vertically upward at a height of 1.5 m above the ground (Fig. 2–31). When you quickly move the nozzle away from the vertical, you hear the water striking the ground next to you for another 2.0 s. What is the water speed as it leaves the nozzle?

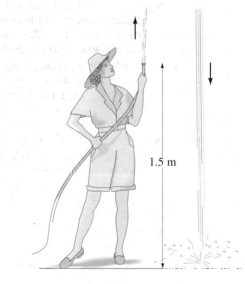

FIGURE 2–31   Problem 48.

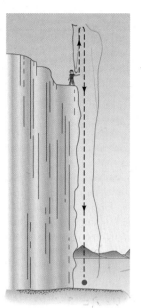

FIGURE 2-32
Problem 49.

49. (III) A stone is thrown vertically upward with a speed of 12.0 m/s from the edge of a cliff 75.0 m high (Fig. 2–32). (a) How much later does it reach the bottom of the cliff? (b) What is its speed just before hitting? (c) What total distance did it travel?

50. (III) A baseball is seen to pass upward by a window 25 m above the street with a vertical speed of 12 m/s. If the ball was thrown from the street, (a) what was its initial speed, (b) what altitude does it reach, (c) when was it thrown, and (d) when does it reach the street again?

* **SECTION 2–8**

* 51. (I) The position of a rabbit along a straight tunnel as a function of time is plotted in Fig. 2–26. What is its instantaneous velocity (a) at $t = 10.0$ s and (b) at $t = 30.0$ s? What is its average velocity (c) between $t = 0$ and $t = 5.0$ s, (d) between $t = 25.0$ s and $t = 30.0$ s, and (e) between $t = 40.0$ s and $t = 50.0$ s?

* 52. (I) In Fig. 2–26, (a) during what time periods, if any, is the object's velocity constant? (b) At what time is its velocity the greatest? (c) At what time, if any, is the velocity zero? (d) Does the object run in one direction or in both along its tunnel during the time shown?

* 53. (I) Figure 2–27 shows the velocity of a train as a function of time. (a) At what time was its velocity greatest? (b) During what periods, if any, was the velocity constant? (c) During what periods, if any, was the acceleration constant? (d) When was the magnitude of the acceleration greatest?

* 54. (II) A high-performance automobile can accelerate approximately as shown in the velocity–time graph of Fig. 2–33. (The short flat spots in the curve represent shifting of the gears.) (a) Estimate the average acceleration of the car in second gear and in fourth gear. (b) Estimate how far the car traveled while in fourth gear.

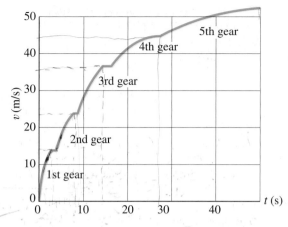

FIGURE 2-33 The velocity of a high-performance automobile as a function of time, starting from a dead stop. The jumps in the curve represent gear shifts. (Problems 54 and 55.)

* 55. (II) Estimate the average acceleration of the car in the previous problem (Fig. 2–33) when it is in (a) first, (b) third, and (c) fifth gear. (d) What is its average acceleration through the first four gears?

* 56. (II) In Fig. 2–27, estimate the distance the object traveled during (a) the first minute and (b) the second minute.

* 57. (II) Construct the v vs. t graph for the object whose displacement as a function of time is given by Fig. 2–26.

* 58. (II) Construct an x vs. t graph for the object whose velocity as a function of time is given by Fig. 2–27.

* 59. (II) Figure 2–34 is a position versus time graph for the motion of an object along the x axis. As the object moves from A to D: (a) Is the object moving in the positive or negative direction? (b) Is the object speeding up or slowing down? (c) Is the acceleration of the object positive or negative? Next, for the time interval from D to E: (d) Is the object moving in the positive or negative direction? (e) Is the object speeding up or slowing down? (f) Is the acceleration of the object positive or negative? (g) Finally, answer these same three questions for the time interval from C to D.

FIGURE 2-34 Problem 59.

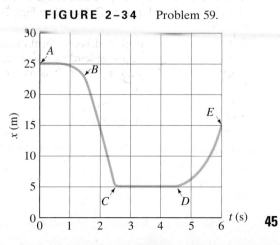

60. A person jumps from a fourth-story window 15.0 m above a firefighter's safety net. The survivor stretches the net 1.0 m before coming to rest, Fig. 2–35. (a) What was the average deceleration experienced by the survivor when slowed to rest by the net? (b) What would you do to make it "safer" (that is, generate a smaller deceleration): would you stiffen or loosen the net? Explain.

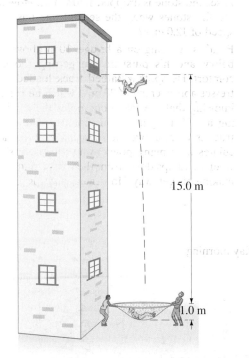

15.0 m

1.0 m

FIGURE 2–35   Problem 60.

61. The acceleration due to gravity on the Moon is about one sixth what it is on Earth. If an object is thrown vertically upward on the Moon, how many times higher will it go than it would on Earth, assuming the same initial velocity?

62. A person who is properly constrained by an over-the-shoulder seat belt has a good chance of surviving a car collision if the deceleration does not exceed 30 "g's" (1.00 g = 9.80 m/s^2). Assuming uniform deceleration of this value, calculate the distance over which the front end of the car must be designed to collapse if a crash brings the car to rest from 100 km/h.

63. A race car driver must average 200.0 km/h over the course of a time trial lasting ten laps. If the first nine laps were done at 199.0 km/h, what average speed must be maintained for the last lap?

64. A car manufacturer tests its cars for front-end collisions by hauling them up on a crane and dropping them from a certain height. (a) Show that the speed just before a car hits the ground, after falling from rest a vertical distance H, is given by $\sqrt{2gH}$. What height corresponds to a collision at (b) 50 km/h? (c) 100 km/h?

65. A first stone is dropped from the roof of a building. 2.00 s after that, a second stone is thrown straight down with an initial speed of 30.0 m/s, and it is observed that the two stones land at the same time. (a) How long did it take the first stone to reach the ground? (b) How high is the building? (c) What are the speeds of the two stones just before they hit the ground?

66. A 90-m-long train begins uniform acceleration from rest. The front of the train has a speed of 20 m/s when it passes a railway worker who is standing 180 m from where the front of the train started. What will be the speed of the last car as it passes the worker? (See Fig. 2–36.)

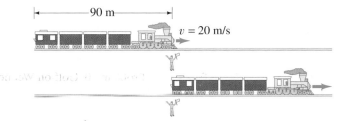

90 m

$v = 20$ m/s

FIGURE 2–36   Problem 66.

67. A police car at rest, passed by a speeder traveling at a constant 110 km/h, takes off in hot pursuit. The police officer catches up to the speeder in 700 m, maintaining a constant acceleration. (a) Qualitatively plot the position versus time graph for both cars from the police car's start to the catch-up point. (b) Calculate how long it took the police officer to overtake the speeder, (c) calculate the required police car acceleration, and (d) calculate the speed of the police car at the overtaking point.

68. In the design of a rapid transit system, it is necessary to balance out the average speed of a train against the distance between stops. The more stops there are, the slower the train's average speed. To get an idea of this problem, calculate the time it takes a train to make a 36-km trip in two situations: (a) the stations at which the trains must stop are 0.80 km apart; and (b) the stations are 3.0 km apart. Assume that at each station the train accelerates at a rate of 1.1 m/s^2 until it reaches 90 km/h, then stays at this speed until its brakes are applied for arrival at the next station, at which time it decelerates at −2.0 m/s^2. Assume it stops at each intermediate station for 20 s.

69. Pelicans tuck their wings and free fall straight down when diving for fish. Suppose a pelican starts its dive from a height of 16.0 m and cannot change its path once committed. If it takes a fish 0.20 s to perform evasive action, at what minimum height must it spot the pelican to escape? Assume the fish is at the surface of the water.

70. In putting, the force with which a golfer strikes a ball is planned so that the ball will stop within some small distance of the cup, say 1.0 m long or short, in case the putt is missed. Accomplishing this from an uphill lie (that is, putting downhill, see Fig. 2–37) is more difficult than from a downhill lie. To see why, assume that on a particular green the ball decelerates constantly at $2.0 \, \text{m/s}^2$ going downhill, and constantly at $3.0 \, \text{m/s}^2$ going uphill. Suppose we have an uphill lie 7.0 m from the cup. Calculate the allowable range of initial velocities we may impart to the ball so that it stops in the range 1.0 m short to 1.0 m long of the cup. Do the same for a downhill lie 7.0 m from the cup. What in your results suggests that the downhill putt is more difficult?

71. A car is behind a truck going 25 m/s on the highway. The driver looks for an opportunity to pass, guessing that his car can accelerate at $1.0 \, \text{m/s}^2$, and he gauges that he has to cover the 20-m length of the truck, plus 10 m clear room at the rear of the truck and 10 m more at the front of it. In the oncoming lane, he sees a car approaching, probably also traveling at 25 m/s. He estimates that the car is about 400 m away. Should he attempt the pass? Give details.

72. A stone is dropped from the roof of a high building. A second stone is dropped 1.50 s later. How far apart are the stones when the second one has reached a speed of 12.0 m/s?

73. Bond is standing on a bridge, 10 m above the road below, and his pursuers are getting too close for comfort. He spots a flatbed truck loaded with mattresses approaching at 30 m/s, which he measures by knowing that the telephone poles the truck is passing are 20 m apart in this country. The bed of the truck is 1.5 m above the road, and Bond quickly calculates how many poles away the truck should be when he jumps down from the bridge onto the truck, making his getaway. How many poles is it?

FIGURE 2–37 Problem 70. Golf on Wednesday morning.

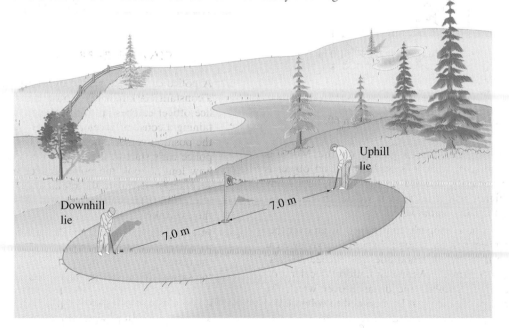

This multiflash photograph of a ping pong ball shows examples of motion in two dimensions. The arcs of the ping pong ball are parabolas that represent "projectile motion." Galileo analyzed projectile motion into its horizontal and vertical components, under the action of gravity (the gold arrow represents the downward acceleration of gravity, **g**).

3 KINEMATICS IN TWO DIMENSIONS; VECTORS

FIGURE 3–1 Car traveling on a road. The green arrows represent the velocity vector at each position.

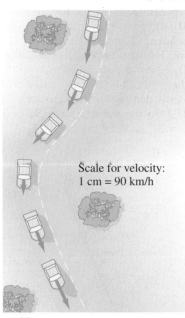

Scale for velocity:
1 cm = 90 km/h

In Chapter 2 we dealt with motion along a straight line. We now consider the description of the motion of objects that move in paths in two (or three) dimensions. To do so we first need to discuss vectors and how they are added.

3–1 Vectors and Scalars

We mentioned in Chapter 2 that the term *velocity* refers not only to how fast something is moving but also to its direction. A quantity such as velocity, which has *direction* as well as *magnitude*, is a **vector** quantity. Other quantities that are also vectors are displacement, force, and momentum. However, many quantities such as mass, time, and temperature have no direction associated with them. They are specified completely by giving a number and units. Such quantities are called **scalars**.

Drawing a diagram of a particular physical situation is always helpful in physics, and this is especially true when dealing with vectors. On a diagram, each vector is represented by an arrow. The arrow is always drawn so that it points in the direction of the vector it represents. The length of the arrow is drawn proportional to the magnitude of the vector. For example, in Fig. 3–1, arrows have been drawn representing the velocity of a car at various places as it rounds a curve. The magnitude of the velocity at each point can be read off this figure by measuring the length of the corresponding arrow and using the scale shown (1 cm = 90 km/h).

When we write the symbol for a vector, we will always use boldface type. Thus for velocity we write **v**. (In handwritten work, the symbol for a vector can be indicated by putting an arrow over it, a $\vec{v}$ for velocity.) If we are concerned only with the magnitude of the vector, we will write simply v, in italics.

3–2 Addition of Vectors—Graphical Methods

Because vectors are quantities that have direction as well as magnitude, they must be added in a special way. In this chapter, we will deal mainly with displacement vectors (for which we now use the symbol **D**) and velocity vectors (**v**). But the results will apply for other vectors we encounter later.

We use simple arithmetic for adding scalars. Simple arithmetic can also be used for adding vectors if they are in the same direction. For example, if a person walks 8 km east one day, and 6 km east the next day, the person will be 8 km + 6 km = 14 km east of the point of origin. We say that the *net* or *resultant* displacement is 14 km to the east (Fig. 3–2a). If, on the other hand, the person walks 8 km east on the first day, and 6 km west (in the reverse direction) on the second day, then the person will end up 2 km from the origin (Fig. 3–2b), so the resultant displacement is 2 km to the east. In this case, the resultant displacement is obtained by subtraction: 8 km − 6 km = 2 km.

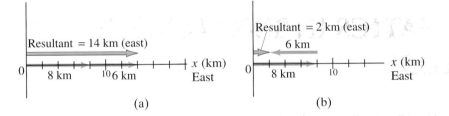

(a)   (b)

FIGURE 3–2 Combining vectors in one dimension.

But simple arithmetic cannot be used if the two vectors are not along the same line. For example, suppose a person walks 10.0 km east and then walks 5.0 km north. These displacements can be represented on a graph in which the positive y axis points north and the positive x axis points east, Fig. 3–3. On this graph, we draw an arrow, labeled **D₁**, to represent the displacement vector of the 10.0-km displacement to the east. Then we draw a second arrow, **D₂**, to represent the 5.0-km displacement to the north. Both vectors are drawn to scale, as in Fig. 3–3.

After taking this walk, the person is now 10.0 km east and 5.0 km north of the point of origin. The **resultant displacement** is represented by the arrow labeled **D_R** in Fig. 3–3. Using a ruler and a protractor, you can measure on this diagram that the person is 11.2 km from the origin at an angle of 27° north of east. In other words, the resultant displacement vector has a magnitude of 11.2 km and makes an angle $\theta = 27°$ with the positive x axis. The magnitude (length) of **D_R** can also be obtained using the theorem of Pythagoras in this case, since D_1, D_2, and D_R form a right triangle with D_R as the hypotenuse. Thus

$$D_R = \sqrt{D_1^2 + D_2^2} = \sqrt{(10.0 \text{ km})^2 + (5.0 \text{ km})^2} = \sqrt{125 \text{ km}^2} = 11.2 \text{ km}.$$

You can use the Pythagorean theorem, of course, only when the vectors are *perpendicular* to each other.

FIGURE 3–3 A person walks 10.0 km east and then 5.0 km north. These two displacements are represented by the vectors **D₁** and **D₂**, which are shown as arrows. The resultant displacement vector, **D_R**, which is the vector sum of **D₁** and **D₂**, is also shown. Measurement on the graph with ruler and protractor shows that **D_R** has a magnitude of 11.2 km and points at an angle $\theta = 27°$ north of east.

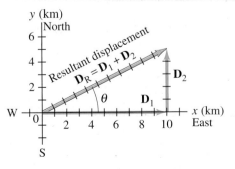

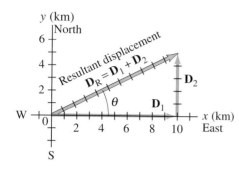

FIGURE 3–3 (Repeated from previous page.) A person walks 10.0 km east and then 5.0 km north. The resultant vector has magnitude $D_R = 11.2$ km at an angle $\theta = 27°$ north of east.

Tail-to-tip method

of

adding vectors

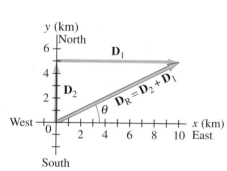

FIGURE 3–4 If the vectors are added in reverse order, the resultant is the same. (Compare Fig. 3–3.)

The resultant displacement vector, $\mathbf{D}_R$, is the sum of the vectors $\mathbf{D}_1$ and $\mathbf{D}_2$. That is,

$$\mathbf{D}_R = \mathbf{D}_1 + \mathbf{D}_2.$$

This is a *vector* equation. An important feature of adding two vectors that are not along the same line is that the magnitude of the resultant vector is not equal to the sum of the magnitudes of the two separate vectors, but is smaller than their sum:

$$D_R < D_1 + D_2. \qquad \text{[Vectors not along the same line]}$$

In our example (Fig. 3–3), $D_R = 11.2$ km, whereas $D_1 + D_2$ equals 15 km. We generally are not interested in $D_1 + D_2$; rather we are interested in the *vector* sum of the two vectors and its magnitude, D_R. Note also that we cannot set $\mathbf{D}_R$ equal to 11.2 km, because we have a vector equation and 11.2 km is only a part of the resultant vector, its magnitude. We could write something like this, though: $\mathbf{D}_R = \mathbf{D}_1 + \mathbf{D}_2 = (11.2 \text{ km}, 27° \text{ N of E})$.

Figure 3–3 illustrates the general rules for graphically adding two vectors together, no matter what angles they make, to get their sum. The rules are as follows:

1. On a diagram, draw one of the vectors—call it $\mathbf{V}_1$—to scale.
2. Next draw the second vector, $\mathbf{V}_2$, to scale, placing its tail at the tip of the first vector and being sure its direction is correct.
3. The arrow drawn from the tail of the first vector to the tip of the second represents the *sum*, or **resultant**, of the two vectors.

Note that vectors can be translated parallel to themselves to accomplish these manipulations. The length of the resultant can be measured with a ruler and compared to the scale. Angles can be measured with a protractor. This method is known as the **tail-to-tip method of adding vectors**.

Note that it is not important in which order the vectors are added. For example, a displacement of 5.0 km north, to which is added a displacement of 10.0 km east, yields a resultant of 11.2 km and angle $\theta = 27°$ (see Fig. 3–4), the same as when they were added in reverse order (Fig. 3–3). That is,

$$\mathbf{V}_1 + \mathbf{V}_2 = \mathbf{V}_2 + \mathbf{V}_1.$$

The tail-to-tip method of adding vectors can be extended to three or more vectors. The resultant is drawn from the tail of the first vector to the tip of the last one added. An example is shown in Fig. 3–5; the three vectors could represent displacements (northeast, south, west) or perhaps three forces. Check for yourself that you get the same resultant no matter in which order you add the three vectors.

FIGURE 3–5
The resultant of three vectors, $\mathbf{V}_R = \mathbf{V}_1 + \mathbf{V}_2 + \mathbf{V}_3$.

A second way to add two vectors is the **parallelogram method**. It is fully equivalent to the tail-to-tip method. In this method, the two vectors are drawn starting from a common origin, and a parallelogram is constructed using these two vectors as adjacent sides as shown in Fig. 3–6b. The resultant is the diagonal drawn from the common origin. In Fig. 3–6a, the tail-to-tip method is shown, and it is clear that both methods yield the same result. It is a common error to draw the sum vector as the diagonal running between the tips of the two vectors, as in Fig. 3–6c. *This is incorrect*: it does not represent the sum of the two vectors. (In fact, it represents their difference, $V_2 - V_1$, as we will see in the next Section.)

Parallelogram method of adding vectors

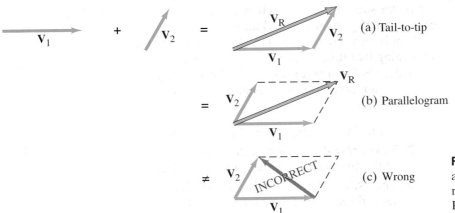

(a) Tail-to-tip

(b) Parallelogram

(c) Wrong

FIGURE 3–6 Vector addition by two different methods, (a) and (b). Part (c) is incorrect.

3–3 Subtraction of Vectors, and Multiplication of a Vector by a Scalar

Given a vector V, we define the *negative* of this vector $(-V)$ to be a vector with the same magnitude as V but opposite in direction, Fig. 3–7. Note, however, that no vector is ever negative in the sense of its magnitude: the magnitude of every vector is positive. A minus sign tells us about its direction.

We can now define the subtraction of one vector from another: the difference between two vectors, $V_2 - V_1$ is defined as

$$V_2 - V_1 = V_2 + (-V_1).$$

That is, the difference between two vectors is equal to the sum of the first plus the negative of the second. Thus our rules for addition of vectors can be applied as shown in Fig. 3–8 using the tail-to-tip method.

FIGURE 3–7 The negative of a vector is a vector having the same length but opposite direction.

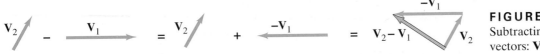

FIGURE 3–8 Subtracting two vectors: $V_2 - V_1$.

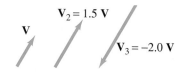

FIGURE 3–9 Multiplying a vector **V** by a scalar *c* gives a vector whose magnitude is *c* times greater and in the same direction as **V** (or opposite direction if *c* is negative).

A vector **V** can be multiplied by a scalar *c*. We define this product so that *c***V** has the same direction as **V** and has magnitude *cV*. That is, multiplication of a vector by a positive scalar *c* changes the magnitude of the vector by a factor *c* but doesn't alter the direction. If *c* is a negative scalar, the magnitude of the product *c***V** is still *cV* (without the minus sign), but the direction is precisely opposite to that of **V**. See Fig. 3–9.

3–4 Adding Vectors by Components

Adding vectors graphically using a ruler and protractor is often not sufficiently accurate and is not useful for vectors in three dimensions. We discuss now a more powerful and precise method for adding vectors.

Consider first a vector **V** that lies in a particular plane. It can be expressed as the sum of two other vectors, called the **components** of the original vector. The components are usually chosen to be along two perpendicular directions. *Resolving a vector into components* The process of finding the components is known as **resolving the vector into its components**. An example is shown in Fig. 3–10; the vector **V** could be a displacement vector that points at an angle $\theta = 30°$ north of east, where we have chosen the positive *x* axis to be to the east and the positive *y* axis north. This vector **V** is resolved into its *x* and *y* components by drawing dashed lines from the tip (*A*) of the vector and drawing these lines perpendicular to the *x* and *y* axes (lines *AB* and *AC*). Then the lines *OB* and *OC* represent the *x* and *y* components of **V**, respectively, as shown in Fig. 3–10b. These *vector components* are written *Vector components* **V**$_x$ and **V**$_y$. We generally show vector components as arrows, like vectors, but dashed. The *scalar components*, V_x and V_y, are numbers, with units, that are given a positive or negative sign depending on whether they point along the positive or negative *x* or *y* axis. As can be seen in Fig. 3–10, **V**$_x$ + **V**$_y$ = **V** by the parallelogram method of adding vectors.

FIGURE 3–10 Resolving a vector **V** into its components along an arbitrarily chosen set of *x* and *y* axes. Note that the components, once found, themselves represent the vector. That is, the components contain as much information as the vector itself.

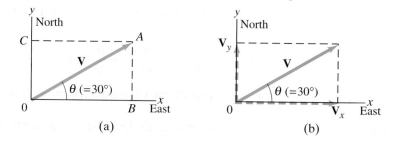

(a)   (b)

Space is made up of three dimensions, and sometimes it is necessary to resolve a vector into components along three mutually perpendicular directions. In rectangular coordinates the components are **V**$_x$, **V**$_y$, and **V**$_z$. Resolution of a vector in three dimensions is merely an extension of the above technique. We will mainly be concerned with situations in which the vectors are in a plane and two components are all that are necessary.

In order to add vectors using the method of components, we need to use the trigonometric functions sine, cosine, and tangent, which we now review.

Given any angle, θ, as in Fig. 3–11a, a right triangle can be constructed by drawing a line perpendicular to either of its sides, as in Fig. 3–11b. The longest side of a right triangle, opposite the right angle, is called the hypotenuse, which we label *h*. The side opposite the angle θ is labeled *o*, and the side adjacent is labeled *a*. We let *h*, *o*, and *a* represent the lengths of these sides, respectively. We now define the three trigonometric functions, sine, cosine, and

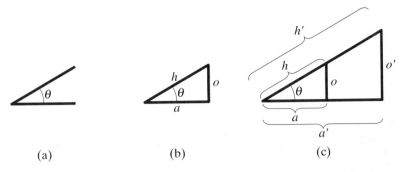

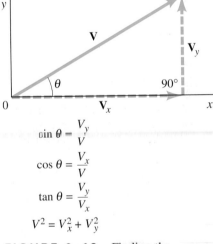

(a) (b) (c)

FIGURE 3-11 Starting with an angle θ as in (a), we can construct right triangles of different sizes, (b) and (c), but the ratio of the lengths of the sides does not depend on the size of the triangle.

tangent (abbreviated sin, cos, tan), in terms of the right triangle, as follows:

$$\sin \theta = \frac{\text{side opposite}}{\text{hypotenuse}} = \frac{o}{h}$$

$$\cos \theta = \frac{\text{side adjacent}}{\text{hypotenuse}} = \frac{a}{h} \qquad \textbf{(3-1)}$$

$$\tan \theta = \frac{\text{side opposite}}{\text{side adjacent}} = \frac{o}{a}.$$

Trig. functions defined

Now it is an interesting fact that if we make the triangle bigger, but keep the same angles, then the ratio of the length of one side to the other, or of one side to the hypotenuse, remains the same. That is, in Fig. 3–11c we have: $a/h = a'/h'$; $o/h = o'/h'$; and $o/a = o'/a'$. Thus the values of sine, cosine, and tangent do not depend on how big the triangle is. They depend only on the size of the angle. The values of sine, cosine, and tangent for different angles can be found using a scientific calculator, or from Tables (see inside rear cover).

A useful trigonometric identity is

$$\sin^2 \theta + \cos^2 \theta = 1 \qquad \textbf{(3-2)}$$

which follows from the Pythagorean theorem ($o^2 + a^2 = h^2$ in Fig. 3–11). That is:

$$\sin^2 \theta + \cos^2 \theta = \frac{o^2}{h^2} + \frac{a^2}{h^2} = \frac{o^2 + a^2}{h^2} = \frac{h^2}{h^2} = 1.$$

(See also Appendix A for other details on trigonometric functions and identities.)

The use of trigonometric functions for finding the components of a vector is illustrated in Fig. 3–12, where it is seen that a vector and its two components can be thought of as making up a right triangle. We then see that the sine, cosine, and tangent are as given in the figure. If we multiply the definition of $\sin \theta = V_y/V$ by V on both sides, we get

$$V_y = V \sin \theta. \qquad \textbf{(3-3a)}$$

Similarly, from the definition of $\cos \theta$, we obtain

$$V_x = V \cos \theta. \qquad \textbf{(3-3b)}$$

Components of a vector

Note that θ is chosen (by convention) to be the angle that the vector makes with the positive x axis.[†]

$$\sin \theta = \frac{V_y}{V}$$

$$\cos \theta = \frac{V_x}{V}$$

$$\tan \theta = \frac{V_y}{V_x}$$

$$V^2 = V_x^2 + V_y^2$$

FIGURE 3-12 Finding the components of a vector using trigonometric functions.

[†]Whatever convention is used, the vector component opposite the angle is proportional to the sine, whether we call that component x or y. Most often we use the convention that it is the y component (Eq. 3–3a).

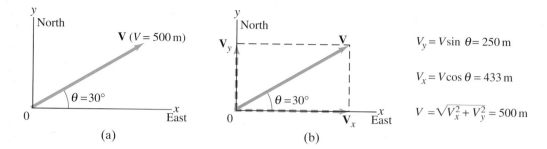

FIGURE 3–13 (a) Vector **V** represents a displacement of 500 m at a 30° angle north of east. (b) The components of **V** are V_x and V_y whose magnitudes are given on the right.

Using Eqs. 3–3, we can calculate V_x and V_y for any vector, such as that illustrated in Fig. 3–10 or Fig. 3–12. Suppose **V** represents a displacement of 500 m in a direction 30° north of east, as shown in Fig. 3–13. Then $V = 500$ m. From the trigonometric tables, sin 30° = 0.500 and cos 30° = 0.866. Then

$$V_x = V \cos \theta = (500 \text{ m})(0.866) = 433 \text{ m (east)},$$

$$V_y = V \sin \theta = (500 \text{ m})(0.500) = 250 \text{ m (north)}.$$

Note that there are two ways to specify a vector in a given coordinate system:

Two ways to specify a vector

1. We can give its components, V_x and V_y.

2. We can give its magnitude V and the angle θ it makes with the positive x axis.

We can shift from one description to the other using Eqs. 3–3, and, for the reverse, by using the theorem of Pythagoras[†] and the definition of tangent:

Components related to magnitude and direction

$$V = \sqrt{V_x^2 + V_y^2} \tag{3–4a}$$

$$\tan \theta = \frac{V_y}{V_x} \tag{3–4b}$$

as can be seen in Fig. 3–12.

We can now discuss how to add vectors using components. The first step is to resolve each vector into its components. Next we can see, using Fig. 3–14,

[†]In three dimensions, the theorem of Pythagoras becomes $V = \sqrt{V_x^2 + V_y^2 + V_z^2}$, where V_z is the component along the third, or z, axis.

FIGURE 3–14
The components of
$\mathbf{V} = \mathbf{V}_1 + \mathbf{V}_2$ are
$V_x = V_{1x} + V_{2x}$ and
$V_y = V_{1y} + V_{2y}$.

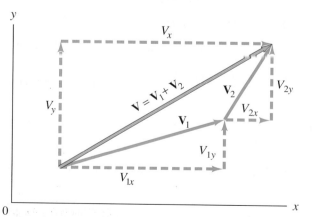

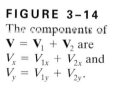

that the addition of any two vectors $\mathbf{V}_1$ and $\mathbf{V}_2$ to give a resultant, $\mathbf{V} = \mathbf{V}_1 + \mathbf{V}_2$, implies that

$$V_x = V_{1x} + V_{2x}$$
$$V_y = V_{1y} + V_{2y}.$$

(3–5)

Adding vectors analytically (by components)

That is, the sum of the x components equals the x component of the result-ant, and similarly for y. That this is valid can be verified by a careful exami-nation of Fig. 3–14. But note carefully that we add all the x components together to get the x component of the resultant; and we add all the y com-ponents together to get the y component of the resultant. We do *not* add x components to y components.

If the magnitude and direction of the resultant vector are desired, they can be obtained using Eqs. 3–4.

The choice of coordinate axes is, of course, always arbitrary. You can often reduce the work involved in adding vectors by a good choice of axes—for example, by choosing one of the axes to be in the same direction as one of the vectors. Then that vector will have only one nonzero component.

Choice of axes can simplify effort needed

EXAMPLE 3–1 **Mail carrier's displacement.** A rural mail carrier leaves the post office and drives 22.0 km in a northerly direction to the next town. She then drives in a direction 60.0° south of east for 47.0 km (Fig. 3–15a) to another town. What is her displacement from the post office?

SOLUTION We want to find her resultant displacement from the origin. We choose the positive x axis to be east and the positive y axis north, and resolve each displacement vector into its components (Fig. 3–15b). Since $\mathbf{D}_1$ has magnitude 22.0 km and points north, it has only a y component:

$$D_{1x} = 0, \quad D_{1y} = 22.0 \text{ km}$$

whereas $\mathbf{D}_2$ has both x and y components:

$$D_{2x} = +(47.0 \text{ km})(\cos 60°) = +(47.0 \text{ km})(0.500) = +23.5 \text{ km}$$
$$D_{2y} = -(47.0 \text{ km})(\sin 60°) = -(47.0 \text{ km})(0.866) = -40.7 \text{ km}.$$

Notice that D_{2y} is negative because this vector component points along the negative y axis. The resultant vector, $\mathbf{D}$, has components:

$$D_x = D_{1x} + D_{2x} = \quad 0 \text{ km} + \quad 23.5 \text{ km} = +23.5 \text{ km}$$
$$D_y = D_{1y} + D_{2y} = 22.0 \text{ km} + (-40.7 \text{ km}) = -18.7 \text{ km}.$$

This specifies the resultant vector completely:

$$D_x = 23.5 \text{ km}, \quad D_y = -18.7 \text{ km}.$$

We can also specify the resultant vector by giving its magnitude and angle using Eqs. 3–4:

$$D = \sqrt{D_x^2 + D_y^2} = \sqrt{(23.5 \text{ km})^2 + (-18.7 \text{ km})^2} = 30.0 \text{ km}$$

$$\tan \theta = \frac{D_y}{D_x} = \frac{-18.7 \text{ km}}{23.5 \text{ km}} = -0.796.$$

A calculator with an INV TAN or TAN^{-1} key gives $\theta = \tan^{-1}(-0.796) = -38.5°$. The negative sign means $\theta = 38.5°$ below the x axis, Fig. 3–15c.

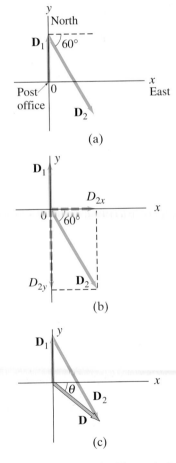

FIGURE 3–15 Example 3–1.

SECTION 3–4 Adding Vectors by Components **55**

The signs of trigonometric functions depend on which "quadrant" the angle falls in: for example, the tangent is positive in the first and third quadrants (from 0° to 90°, and 180° to 270°), but negative in the second and fourth quadrants; see Appendix A–8. The best way to keep track of angles, and to check any vector result, is always to draw a vector diagram. A vector diagram gives you something tangible to look at when analyzing a problem, and provides a check on the results.

Here is a brief summary of how to add two or more vectors using components:

1. Draw a diagram, adding the vectors graphically.

2. Choose x and y axes. Choose them in a way, if possible, that will make your work easier. (For example, choose one axis along the direction of one of the vectors so that vector will have only one component.)

3. Resolve each vector into its x and y components, showing each component along its appropriate (x or y) axis as a (dashed) arrow.

4. Calculate each component (when not given) using sines and cosines. If θ_1 is the angle vector $\mathbf{V}_1$ makes with the x axis, then:

$$V_{1x} = V_1 \cos \theta_1, \qquad V_{1y} = V_1 \sin \theta_1.$$

Pay careful attention to signs: any component that points along the negative x or y axis gets a negative sign.

5. Add the x components together to get the x component of the resultant. Ditto for y:

$$V_x = V_{1x} + V_{2x} + \text{any others}$$

$$V_y = V_{1y} + V_{2y} + \text{any others.}$$

This is the answer: the components of the resultant vector.

6. If you want to know the magnitude and direction of the resultant vector, use Eqs. 3–4:

$$V = \sqrt{V_x^2 + V_y^2}, \qquad \tan \theta = \frac{V_y}{V_x}.$$

The vector diagram you already drew helps to obtain the correct position (quadrant) of the angle θ.

EXAMPLE 3–2 **Three short trips.** An airplane trip involves three legs, with two stopovers, as shown in Fig. 3–16a. The first leg is due east for 620 km; the second leg is southeast (45°) for 440 km; and the third leg is at 53° south of west, for 550 km, as shown. What is the plane's total displacement?

FIGURE 3–16
Example 3–2.

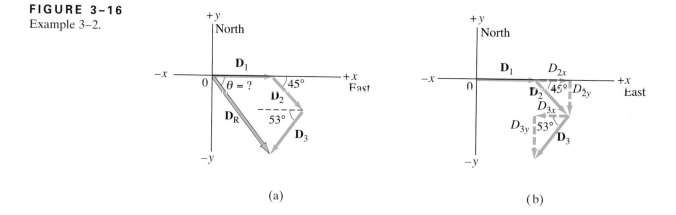

(a)

(b)

SOLUTION We follow the steps in the above Problem Solving box:
(1) and (2): Already shown in Fig. 3–16a, where we have taken the x axis as east (then $\mathbf{D}_1$ has only an x component).
(3): It is imperative to draw a good figure. The components are shown in Fig. 3–16b. Notice that instead of drawing all the vectors starting from a common origin, as we did in Fig. 3–15b, here we have drawn them "tail-to-tip" style, which is just as valid and may make it easier to see.
(4) Now we calculate the components:

$$\mathbf{D}_1: D_{1x} = +D_1 \cos 0° = D_1 = 620 \text{ km}$$
$$D_{1y} = +D_1 \sin 0° = 0 \text{ km}$$
$$\mathbf{D}_2: D_{2x} = +D_2 \cos 45° = +(440 \text{ km})(0.707) = +311 \text{ km}$$
$$D_{2y} = -D_2 \sin 45° = -(440 \text{ km})(0.707) = -311 \text{ km}$$
$$\mathbf{D}_3: D_{3x} = -D_3 \cos 53° = -(550 \text{ km})(0.602) = -331 \text{ km}$$
$$D_{3y} = -D_3 \sin 53° = -(550 \text{ km})(0.799) = -439 \text{ km.}$$

Note carefully that we have given a minus sign to each component that in Fig. 3–16b points in the negative x or negative y direction. We see why a good drawing is so important. We summarize the components in the table in the margin.
(5): This is easy:

Vector	Components	
	x (km)	y (km)
$\mathbf{D}_1$	620	0
$\mathbf{D}_2$	311	-311
$\mathbf{D}_3$	-331	-439
$\mathbf{D}_R$	600	-750

$$D_x = D_{1x} + D_{2x} + D_{3x} = 620 \text{ km} + 311 \text{ km} - 331 \text{ km} = \quad 600 \text{ km}$$
$$D_y = D_{1y} + D_{2y} + D_{3y} = \quad 0 \text{ km} - 311 \text{ km} - 439 \text{ km} = -750 \text{ km.}$$

The x and y components are 600 km and -750 km, and point respectively to the east and south. This is one way to give the answer.
(6): We can also give the answer as

$$D_R = \sqrt{D_x^2 + D_y^2} = \sqrt{(600)^2 + (-750)^2} \text{ km} = 960 \text{ km}$$

$$\tan\theta = \frac{D_y}{D_x} = \frac{-750 \text{ km}}{600 \text{ km}} = -1.25, \qquad \text{so } \theta = -51°,$$

where we assume only two significant figures. Thus, the total displacement has magnitude 960 km and points 51° below the x axis (south of east), as was shown in our original sketch, Fig. 3–16a.

3–5 Projectile Motion

In Chapter 2, we studied the motion of objects in one dimension in terms of displacement, velocity, and acceleration, including purely vertical motion of falling bodies undergoing acceleration due to gravity. Now we examine the more general motion of objects moving through the air in two dimensions near the Earth's surface, such as a golf ball, a thrown or batted baseball, kicked footballs, speeding bullets, and athletes doing the long jump or high

FIGURE 3–17 This strobe photograph of a soccer ball in the air shows the characteristic "parabolic" path of projectile motion.

jump. These are all examples of **projectile motion** (see Fig. 3–17), which we can describe as taking place in two dimensions. Although air resistance is often important, in many cases its effect can be ignored, and we will ignore it in the following analysis. We will not be concerned now with the process by which the object is thrown or projected. We consider only its motion *after* it has been projected and is moving freely through the air under the action of gravity alone. Thus the acceleration of the object is that due to gravity, which acts downward with magnitude $g = 9.80 \text{ m/s}^2$, and we assume it is constant.[†]

Horizontal and vertical motion analyzed separately

Galileo first accurately described projectile motion. He showed that it could be understood by analyzing the horizontal and vertical components of the motion separately. This was an innovative analysis, not done in this way

[†]This restricts us to objects whose distance traveled and maximum height above the Earth are small compared to the Earth's radius (6400 km).

FIGURE 3–18 Projectile motion. (A vertically falling object is shown at the left for comparison.)

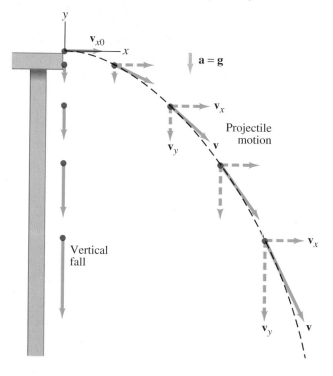